HOW TO

Lindie Naughton is a Dublin journalist, writer and improving gardener.

HOW to MOW the LAWN

GARDENING FOR BEGINNERS

LINDIE NAUGHTON

NEW
ISLAND

Copyright © 2002 Lindie Naughton

HOW TO MOW THE LAWN
First published September 2002
by New Island Books
2 Brookside
Dundrum Road
Dublin 14

The moral right of the author has been asserted.

ISBN 1 904301 07 X

British Library Cataloguing in Publication Data.
A CIP catalogue record for this book is available
from the British Library.

Typeset by New Island
Cover design by Slick Fish
Printed in Ireland by Colour Books Ltd

10 9 8 7 6 5 4 3 2 1

CONTENTS

To my father
Ben Naughton

Introduction

If gardening is the new rock 'n' roll, a lot of us are in big trouble. Come on, own up – do you shrink into inadequacy if forced to watch one of those gardening programmes on television? Do you wish the long Latin names of plants in the garden centre were replaced by something simple, like 'green plant with yellow flower'? Do you recoil in fear at the word 'pruning'?

Outside our houses, most of us have a patch of green, surrounded by neglected earth and embellished by weeds with names we don't know in English, let alone Latin. If we live in an apartment building, we may have a windowsill or a balcony that could do with a plant or two to liven it up. Some of us even have allotments.

The problem is that few of us are born gardeners. We might like to do something with our green space, but we haven't a clue how to start – and the hundreds of books crowding the shelves aren't much help. They all seem to start on chapter four. One book I picked up on organic gardening was full of instructions about how to build cold frames and small sheds. Sorry, lads, but that is what carpenters are for. At the other end of the scale are lavish publications with full colour pictures of curvilinear flowerbeds. These books are as off-putting for the aspiring gardener as the television programmes. Their problem is that they are written by experts for experts. They expect the reader to know far too much.

I know that there are a lot of obsessive gardeners out there. These are people who know exactly what jobs they should be doing in any month of the year to get the perfect effect next May or September. They jam the lines of radio gardening programmes with detailed, intelligent questions. While improving all the time, I am not (yet) one of those people.

When I moved into my suburban house, I knew nothing about gardening. I had vague notions about digging and weeding, but that was about it. I even made a mess of mowing the lawn. This is a skill my gardening friends seem to think we are all born with; believe me, we are not. A few years on, I can take some pride in my garden, although plants still die inexplicably, my fruit trees either won't grow at all or grow too fast and, thanks to a large indigenous population of slugs, attempts at a herb garden and a small vegetable patch have been less than successful.

At least I can keep it all under control and I am getting more skilled. Not that I plan on turning into too much of a fanatic. Gardening is something I prefer to do standing up, rarely in winter and not for more than a couple of hours a week.

I am certain that a lot of you feel exactly the same – while you would like to do a little something with what you've got, you do not have a lot of time. You want to know the basics about watering plants, killing weeds and clipping hedges – the kind of thing everyone needs to know before attempting to buy a plant or sow a seed. If any or all of these supposedly simple tasks are a mystery to you, read on!

Note: *The imperial conversions of metric measurements in this book are rounded up or down to the nearest foot.*

Basic Principles

♦ Keep it simple

♦ Forget about growing from seed
(initially at least)

♦ Don't plant anything before March

♦ Assume that every plant likes the sun
until you find out otherwise

♦ Move and prune in late autumn or
early spring

1. How to Mow the Lawn

You have just moved into your house and, presumably, it's new or has been lying empty for a while. The small patch of green to the front and a larger stretch to the back probably look like unkempt meadows: grass so high it has gone to seed, dandelions waving their golden heads in the wind, out-of-control brambles, mammoth hedges and maybe even a bed or two of nettles (good sign: it means you have rich soil).

The first step is to hack back the jungle. If this is too much of a job, pay a professional gardener to do it. With specialised equipment, he or she will have it cut back in no time. Once this is done, you will most likely be left with an area of neglected grass surrounded by strips of rock-solid, bare earth, later to become the flowerbeds, and a few neglected plants. These are best left until you decide what you want to do. For the moment, you have to cut the grass, and this is the one job for which you emphatically do not need a professional. Anyone is capable of mowing a lawn, right?

Before you start, you need the right equipment: a lawnmower. No problem, you think. Unfortunately, this was far from the case for me, as I soon found out. With the space at the back of my house cleared, I went off to the local DIY superstore to buy a push lawnmower. This would not only do the job, it would also give me some exercise.

The first problem when I got the mower home was putting

the thing together. It came in two parts – the wheels and blades, and then a bent length of metal tubing forming a handle. The two had to be joined with screws. Simple enough. However, try as I might, I could not get the screws tight enough, which meant that the handle buckled under the least pressure. This made the task of mowing a modest back garden tougher and more frustrating than I had expected. It also gave me blistered hands and a sore back. Mowing the lawn became something to dread. I gave up on the manual machine and now use a large petrol rotary mower that occupies a lot of garage space, but gets the job done quickly and efficiently, taking just four minutes for the small front lawn.

So how do you pick the best mower?

Picking the Best Mower

There are three kinds of lawnmower. A *cylinder mower*, whether manual or powered, has a number of moving blades and one fixed one. A bowling-green attendant would shun anything other than a 12-bladed cylinder mower, but these are not suitable for high grass. They are also expensive. A *rotary mower* cuts with a scythe-like action. It is a good all-rounder, though not as fine-cutting as a cylinder. Finally there is the *hover mower*. This consists of a blade rotating at high speed, sitting on a cushion of air built up by a fan beneath the canopy. It can be used in wetter conditions than wheeled machines. Although light, hover mowers are not always easy to control and can be dangerous around children, pets and feet.

Hand vs. Electric vs. Petrol

Lawnmowers can be powered in several ways:

HAND: If you have a small lawn that takes only a few

minutes to cut, a hand mower is probably best and gets a lovely effect.

ELECTRIC: These come in two versions: one has wheels and the other hovers. For both, you need to be close to a source of electricity, making them more suitable for small, suburban gardens.

PETROL: This is the old-fashioned method of powering a lawnmower and the one that most people would think the best. For a start, you do not have to worry about electrocuting yourself on a trailing power line. Petrol mowers are solid machines, and if well maintained will give years of trouble-free service. If you have a huge lawn to look after, you can even get one you can sit on. The only problem is storage even the smallest version can take up a lot of space.

Rotary mower

Hover mower

Cylinder mower

The Art of Mowing

You have your machine and are faced with knee-high grass. The good news is that an efficient lawnmower will power its way through the densest of growth in no time.

The best way to mow a lawn is in stages, patiently and gently. In the past, the first cut of a lawn was done with a scythe to protect the young shoots. Fortunately, technology means that this is now unnecessary because most lawnmowers allow you to adjust the height of the blades. If your mower is electric, make adjustments before you plug it in. NEVER put your fingers anywhere near the blades on any machine! For an overgrown lawn, it's best to leave the blades pretty high at first (at least one notch higher than you think) and then, a couple of days later, when everything has settled, come back and have another go with the blades lowered a couple of notches. An advantage of this method is that the lawnmower will not keep stalling as the blades get clogged with thick grass.

When I started tending my lawn, I thought it best to keep the blades as close as possible to the ground by using the first or second notch. I then wondered why my front garden had the scorched look of an African desert. The problem was that, in the hope of reducing the number of times I had to do the job, I was shaving the grass far too closely. No lawn needs this. Keeping the growth a little higher means that it is more likely to stay a luxuriant green. Another plus is that stubborn weeds are not so obvious.

Be warned: no matter how closely you cut your grass, you will still have to haul out the lawnmower at least once a week and probably twice during the height of the growing season. Try to cut only when the grass is perfectly dry. Not just the cutting but also the impact of the lawnmower wheels on a wet lawn can cause lasting damage.

Edging the Lawn

The grass is immaculately cut with hardly a weed to be seen. But you are not happy; the edges are creeping onto your driveway and flowerbeds. Being inflicted with the tidiness gene, you want it all to look razor sharp.

Like many a fledgling gardener, I bought myself an electric edger. These machines operate by shredding everything in sight by means of a length of plastic string that spins at great speed once the machine is turned on. Because they are small, they can get into corners and other awkward spots. Fine in theory, but I found it did not live up to the publicity. First, the cover fell off and I couldn't get it back on. The result was a fine coating of masticated grass on everything, especially my legs and feet; inevitably, this mess found its way into the house. Then I discovered that the plastic string wore out and needed regular adjustment, a fiddly and tiresome task. On top of these problems, the proximity of a dangerous cutting implement to a power line, that you get with all electric gardening tools, made me nervous. Soon the electric miracle machine was gathering dust, and my garden edges were again straying uncontrollably.

Then, while waiting at the cash register of my local DIY shop, I spotted an unusual round-bladed spade. Its official name was a 'half-moon edger' and it cost just ⊠8. What had I to lose? It turned out to be the most useful tool I have ever bought. You just place it on the edge of the grass and stick a boot on it. As the blade sinks into the soil, the grass folds in on itself. Repeat as you move around the grass edge and, hey presto, you've got a tidy lawn!

Weeding the Lawn

There is an environmental issue when it comes to weed-killing. The chemicals you may be tempted to use for clearing even a small patch of grass will eventually find their way from your soil into the water table. The message is clear: don't use them, even if it that means you must learn to live with a less-than-perfect lawn. Having said that, the sight of a fresh crop of dandelions bursting through my lawn enrages my usually calm soul. Not for one moment is the invader allowed to live. This is irrational behaviour; a weed, after all, is just a plant in the wrong place, and I remain quite fond of daisies, also technically weeds.

The problem with dandelions and daisies is their aggressive sociability: when it comes to reproducing themselves, these weeds are the rabbits of the plant world. One day, you have a single but annoying dandelion; within weeks, it's goodbye lawn. On top of everything else, your neighbours will not thank you for letting your dandelions flourish; this dandelion-hater has been known to sneak into a neglected garden at night to kill a noxious growth of yellow-heads. Unfortunately, weeds, like dandelions, daisies, plantain, moss and a little purple flower I am plagued with, love to hide themselves in the grass; once they get established, it's maddeningly hard to remove them. Adding to the irritation is their perennial nature. Year in year out, they come back, regardless of what you do.

The anti-weed campaign must start early in the year. In the past, I have used those combined weed-and-feed concoctions, which claim to get rid of your weeds and help the grass grow at the same time, mainly because one of them comes in a special container complete with sprinkler, making it easy to use. But apart from being bad for the environment, they are expensive and I am not convinced that they work. It is better to feed as soon as the grass starts to grow in spring, and follow this with a weed-elimination routine. Start all this a few days after making your 'first cut' of the spring season when the problems to be tackled will become very obvious.

Go by the weather rather than the calendar date – there is no point feeding and weeding if it is still freezing cold, even if it is April. Be careful administering the feed, which should be an environmentally friendly nitrogen-rich mixture, easy to find in your local garden centre. Too great a concentration will burn and kill the lawn, leaving an ugly brown patch behind. I don't quite know how to get around this problem as the grains seem to come out of their box or container in a rush or not at all. The experts say to hand-feed, but even then, too much can fly out between your fingers. One solution is to use an ordinary garden broom to sweep the area after feeding and then water thoroughly to dilute the concentration. Another is to use a special lawn sand with a small percentage of added nitrogen. This has the added benefit of smothering moss and some weeds.

For spot-killing of weeds, a type of weedkiller that comes in a bottle with a sponge on top can be dabbed on the weeds individually. Then there are the old-fashioned remedies, also applied directly to the weed. Boiling water straight from the kettle gets rid of daisies overnight, while salt kills off dandelions and much else besides. Like all plants, weeds are mostly composed of water and, as salt sucks away all this fluid, it is worth trying this on any stubborn weed. One of my problems with the front lawn was a growth of plantain, that flat waxy-leafed weed that is as prolific as daisies and completely smothers the grass. I tried a well-known commercial weed-killer. Nothing happened. I then got out the salt-cellar and sprinkled carefully until the plant was lightly covered. By the next day, the plantain had shrivelled away, and, even better, there were no nasty bald patches left behind.

But even salt is best used conservatively as it is not suitable for everything and will not stop a weed reappearing. Carefully removing weeds by hand is without question the best option. A small wooden-handled tool with a long single prong and a tip like a snake's tongue – called a weed-grubber – does the trick for me, removing weeds with very little damage to the surrounding grass.

Moss is the most pernicious of lawn destroyers. It grows in damp shady parts of your garden, beside a wall, for instance, and can also flourish in an old, or tired lawn, especially if the lawn is mown too closely or when the grass is wet. The moss-infected patch needs vigorous and regular raking to remove the growth on top of the lawn and to improve the drainage. Think of it as combing out a head of matted hair. If this doesn't work, a mixture of sand and nitrogen is available from garden centres as a cure for moss. Just scatter it by hand over the grass. Breaking up the soil by sticking a fork into it several times and then adding sand can help improve drainage, but you may find the only solution for persistent moss is to dig up that part of the lawn completely and re-seed it. My inclination would be to use the space for something else because nothing seems to get rid of this menace, especially if that part of your garden is in permanent shade. Think laterally: it could be the ideal site for a garden hut or a piece of sculpture.

Feeding the Lawn

Even the best-kept lawn gets tired and the result is poor growth and yellow, sickly grass. Overuse can also be a problem. There is no doubt that if walked on all the time (think of the goal area on a football pitch), a lawn will suffer. Fortunately, all that tired grass needs is a tonic: in spring, when the grass is just starting to grow, apply one of the many widely available brands of organic lawn fertilizer, usually based on seaweed. If it doesn't rain, give the lawn a watering to help the fertilizer work its way into the soil. A side-effect of this treatment is that weeds will also start to show, so get to work on them as soon as they appear. This remedy should be all that is needed, but if the lawn is still a pale colour in midsummer and you're really fussy, apply another tonic.

It is also worth treating the lawn again in the autumn and special mixtures are available for this time of year. Garden centres will advise you on the best product to buy – the ones recommended for use in autumn are usually more expensive.

Patching Up the Lawn

Occasionally you may have to re-seed your lawn. The first decision you face concerns seed because there are many different kinds of grass. Some types are designed to be tough; others are soft and beautifully lush, but you dare not walk on them. There are specialised grasses for bowling greens, tennis courts and football pitches. Assuming you want a practical rather than an ornamental lawn, choose a utility grass seed that is guaranteed to be hard-wearing and will require little attention, apart from regular mowing. These can be found in any garden centre and are relatively inexpensive.

Before seeding an area, check that it is flat and level with the rest of your lawn. In particular, if a flowerbed or shrub has been removed, there may be a shallow hole, which should be built up with extra soil before you seed. Rake this gently and then smooth it over with a length of wood to check that it is level with the rest of the lawn. Throw the seeds down as evenly as possible; the bare patches will be obvious. Spray gently with water if it hasn't rained, using a watering can with small holes in the sprinkler, or 'rose', to ensure that the seeds are not washed away. Shoots should appear within three weeks.

When you mow a lawn, you will discover areas where the surface is not flat, and you may wish to do something about this. A shallow hollow can be levelled out with a sandy top-dressing (mix some sand and compost in a bucket). Build up the soil level gradually in autumn and winter by sprinkling on thin layers. Once grass has grown through this, add more layers at regular intervals until the lawn is level. To build up a depression or hollow, cut it in an 'H' shape with a half-moon edger and peel back the topsoil and grass like two flaps. Put some extra soil or compost underneath and then cover by rolling the flaps back into their original position. Stamp everything down. To flatten a small bump, do the reverse. Roll back the top carefully as before, but this time, take out some of the soil from underneath with a trowel. Then cover it over again and stamp it down.

Scarifying and Aerating

A good going-over with a rake in September will rid the lawn of dead leaves, weeds and roots and refresh the soil before the colder weather sets in. The technical term for this is 'scarifying', which means scratching the outer surface to increase water absorption and help germination. In the spring, a gentler raking will do much the same job without damaging the surface, which would make the lawn vulnerable to weeds.

As for aeration, or keeping the soil loose and open, if you

have a good population of worms, you won't have to worry about this, although those muddy spirals they throw up, called worm casts, should be removed. When walked on, they spread, making nasty, muddy patches on the lawn. If the surface of your lawn has become compacted – for instance, where children or animals have used it as a short-cut – it may need breaking up. This is best done in autumn by taking a fork and sticking it straight into the ground to a depth of about 7cms (3ins), so breaking up the surface and letting in air and water. Repeat as many times as necessary. In the spring, some gardeners like to use a special spiked roller to 'prick' open the soil's upper layer but a thorough raking in the autumn and a gentler one in the spring should be enough for most lawns.

Dogs and Cats

The scourge of dogs and their leg-cocking antics is just one of the reasons you may have to re-seed a patch of your lawn. Dog urine scorches a lawn and little can be done to prevent or cure it, especially if the dog is your own. Even more annoying are visiting dogs. Once a dog comes, he will return, attracted by his own smell. Watering the area thoroughly will minimise the damage. If the grass refuses to regenerate, re-seeding is the only answer. Cats are just as bad, especially in urban areas, and the smell can be awful. The droppings of wild and domestic animals and birds are also a considerable hazard if young children are using the garden. To keep dogs away, place a bottle half-filled with water in a strategic position. For some reason, this frightens them off. As for cat repellents, there are a number of preparations and devices for sale, while plain white pepper is sometimes recommended. Some herbs are marketed as cat and dog repellents; they work by confusing the animal's sense of smell. They may be worth trying. To discourage unwanted visitors, it is worth remembering the simple solutions, like keeping the garden gates closed.

Buying In

If your house is new, with barely a blade of grass to the front or rear of the building, you can buy an instant lawn, though it will be expensive. This looks good straight away; it is weed-free and can be walked on within a week. If it settles well, you can start your mowing routine about three weeks later. Instant lawn, for which you are charged by the metre, is available from landscape gardeners.

Hot Tips for Your Lawn

- Mow at least once a week in summer.
- Do not shave the lawn too closely.
- Make sure the grass is dry before you mow.
- Feed first and then weed.
- Deal with brown patches, weeds and other problems as soon as they appear.

---

2. The Right Tools for the Job

Before any work gets done, there is the question of finding the right tools. Thousands of years ago, the very first tools were invented in order to tend the earth. A well-shaped stick or stone or shell was much prized. Later, in the Iron Age, came the first shovels and rakes.

Not a lot has changed since then, despite the bewildering array of tools and supposedly labour-saving devices – manual, electric and petrol-driven – available at the local DIY store or garden centre. The temptation is to go mad. You buy not one but two varieties of spade, plus a rake, an electric edger, a wheelbarrow and a long-armed tree-lopper with telescopic handles, only to realise when you get home that your bushes are not that tall and that the wheelbarrow takes up a lot of space.

To keep a good garden, you need very little in the way of tools, although the essentials are worth choosing carefully. Comfort and ease of use is vital, so check anything you buy for weight, balance and that indefinable quality known as 'feel'. Poorly chosen tools result in backaches, blisters and frustration. Well-chosen tools will become good friends that can last a lifetime.

SPADE: There is a difference between a shovel and a spade. A shovel is an instrument for lifting or scooping material such as earth or coal. It consists of a curved metal blade or scoop that looks like a miniature shield attached to a long handle. A spade is a tool for digging, typically consisting of a flat rectangular steel blade attached to a shorter handle.

Spades come in many designs. Some have longer handles for the tall gardener while others come with smaller blades for light work. Some spades have a longer blade, which means they can get under awkward plants easily. Other spades attempt to combine the qualities of a spade and a shovel and are not recommended. The ultimate spade comes in polished stainless steel, making it easy to clean and long-lasting. A good spade is expensive, but worth it. Do shop around as prices can vary dramatically.

RAKE: When your digging is finished, your flowerbed will look as if it has been invaded by a colony of moles. To level it out and break up lumps, you rake the surface. Raking will also help locate the stones and debris that must be removed to create the perfect seedbed.

There are two kinds of rake. The most common looks like a large metal comb attached to a handle. This is used not just for smoothing over your flowerbeds but also for scarifying the lawn in autumn. The other variety, known as a spring-tine rake, has a large fan-like set of flexible prongs and is useful for clearing up dead leaves or hedge clippings.

TROWEL: The trowel is a most versatile tool and the one you will use most often. Resembling a miniature spade, it often comes with a three-pronged fork as an 'indoor plant set'. Mine has a longer handle and blade than most. For working close to plants, where you don't want to upset the roots, a trowel and a hand fork are vital. Buy metal rather than plastic and stainless steel if you can afford it.

FORK: The typical garden fork has four prongs or 'tines' and a number of uses. There is nothing like a fork for breaking

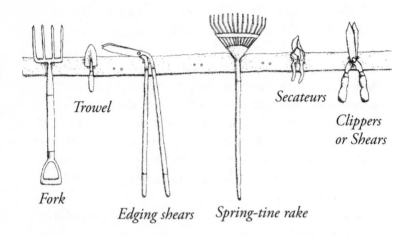

Trowel

Secateurs

*Clippers
or Shears*

Fork

Edging shears   *Spring-tine rake*

up soil, especially after digging, or for opening out a new flowerbed in a grass-covered area. A fork can also be used for moving hedge clippings or old grass and for distributing compost. In spring, sticking it directly into the lawn helps break up compacted soil; there is even a special fork with hollow prongs for this purpose.

HOE: The hoe is often described as our best weapon in the war on weeds. The principle of hoeing is to stop weeds in their early seedling stage, and there is an old saying that if you hoe when there aren't any weeds, you won't get them. So how do you hoe?

'You stick your hoe just under the soil surface, slice through the weed roots and then move on. The earth comes through the hole in the blade,' is how my father describes the art of hoeing. There are two versions of the hoe. The one with the hole in the blade, described above, is known as a Dutch hoe. Another type, a draw hoe, has an angled blade. You walk

18

Dutch hoe

Draw hoe

backwards, pulling as you go. It should be possible to hoe without stooping, so buy one with a handle that reaches eye level. What bothers me about hoeing are the little seedlings that stay on the surface of the soil, which then settle down and start growing again. For this reason, I prefer to hand-weed, although the hoe is useful for getting at awkward spots.

SHEARS: If you have a hedge, you will need to clip it at least twice from April to August – and that is not allowing for global warming and the effect it has on growth; with milder winters, the growing period can continue until early December. A pair of garden shears will do the job nicely and is handy for other cutting jobs. Clipping a hedge by hand does not take as long as you might think and it is good exercise. Hand-clipping is also comparatively safe. Every summer, doctors' surgeries are filled with victims of gardening accidents, and one of the chief culprits is the electric hedge-trimmer. Because they are often used above eye level, these can be difficult to control. Even professional gardeners have problems with them; a friend lost the top of a finger and severed the tendon in another while using one. Petrol machines are safer, as there is no trailing cable, but they can be equally difficult to control.

TRIMMER: Because of aggressive marketing, the electric grass trimmer or 'strimmer' has become almost as popular as the lawnmower, but whether every garden needs one is open to question. The fledgling gardener uses it a couple of times but soon realises that a combination of spade, clippers and a half-moon edger can do the job just as well if not better – and you don't have to fiddle with annoying little spools of plastic string.

SECATEURS: A pair of secateurs, or hand-clippers, is vital for pruning roses and other small bush-type plants. Secateurs cut when squeezed and, with one very sharp blade, need careful storing. They come in several styles, but the most popular have curved blades and are available in several sizes. Buy as good as you can afford; cheap secateurs do not stay sharp and soon fall apart. A medium-sized pair should do most of the usual jobs, though thicker branches on more mature bushes may need a pruning saw, or an axe if low-lying.

WATERING CAN: These used to come in tin but are now mostly plastic and are vital for small-scale watering. You will need a large one for mature plants and a smaller one for seedlings and houseplants. Most watering cans come equipped with a round sprinkling 'rose' on the spout which allows you to spray rather than drown a plant; some come with several different sizes of rose, which is even better. Roses are sold separately in most gardening centres, but finding one that stays on the end of the spout can be difficult, so if possible, test before you buy. Buy an aerosol mister or sprayer while you are at it; these are useful indoors when damping delicate seedlings.

HOSE: A gift for any gardener is an outdoor tap as it allows for easy hosing of the garden. Most of us are not so lucky and have an annual struggle getting the hose to stay attached to the kitchen tap, which is probably a model of modern design but not made to fit garden hoses. For this reason, I have abandoned my hose and, until I get in a plumber to give me an outside tap, will continue to use my watering can. If you do have a hose and want it to last, it is important to store it on its reel when you have finished with the job in hand. That way, it will not develop any kinks and the plastic is less likely to perish.

WHEELBARROW: Whoever invented the wheelbarrow came up with a simple but supremely clever design, involving one wheel and human muscle power. Wheelbarrows can be useful for moving old grass, compost or plants around the garden. But they take up a lot of space, even if you can hang them on a wall, and most gardeners with a small garden will find that a bucket will do just as well.

NEW TOOLS: Now available at your local gardening or DIY centre are gardening tool 'systems'. These consist of a handle, usually in metal, and a collection of various tool heads, such as hoes, rakes and edgers, which you can change as the need arises. Whether they are as strong as a purpose-made tool is open to question. Heavily promoted in recent years is the 'Garden Claw', which twists weeds out of the ground, but is hard on the wrists. You may also find a flame-throwing weed-killing rod, which spot-burns weeds, worth considering.

Other Bits and Pieces

Even the most casual of gardeners will need lots of small items, such as pegs, string, plant labels and pens. I also find all sorts of uses for an ordinary kitchen fork; lifting delicate seedlings for instance. Tip: keep everything small in the transparent plastic boxes you get in the supermarket when you buy soft fruit like plums or strawberries.

Looking after Tools

Well-kept tools can last forever. Obviously, it is a good idea to clean and dry tools after use, getting rid of clumps of grass and earth. Shears and secateurs should be oiled regularly and the blades wiped with an oily rag. Tools with cutting edges need occasional sharpening. If possible, hang your tools on a wall – a piece of wood and a few large nails can make a functional rack.

Dressing for the Garden

Gardening is dirty work, so you have to dress appropriately. Keep an old pair of trousers and shoes for this purpose. Never wear good shoes even if all you're planning is a small bit of weeding. You would be amazed at how filthy a pair of shoes can get in five minutes. If hosing or watering, rubber boots are probably a good idea. If you are using electric tools, wear protective clothing and goggles, and heavy boots when appropriate.

You may or may not wish to wear gardening gloves. There are many varieties available across a wide price range. Some, in suede, are useful for dealing with roses and other thorny shrubs; others, with reinforced rubber fingers, make dirty jobs easier on the hands. But most garden gloves are ill-fitting and give you no feel for what you are doing. I do without most of the time, but after a scare a few years ago when my eyes streamed badly after a weeding session, I always use a pair of thick rubber gloves for hand-weeding.

Safety

All tools can cause damage, especially those with sharp blades. A lawnmower can chop off fingers in double-quick time, and most people will have the common sense to ensure that any cutting machine is turned off properly before going near the blades, even if just to remove old grass. It is worth being even more careful. On my petrol lawnmower, for instance, even after the engine has cut out, I always pull out the sparkplug before turning the machine on its side to examine the innards. Otherwise, the blade may still kick around.

Potentially the most lethal are the electric power tools now proliferating in garden centres. Chainsaws, rotivators, shredders and high-power hedge-trimmers can all be bought or hired, although I think they are best left to the professionals. But if you feel happy using them, play safe by keeping a close watch on the power line and making sure it stays untangled and as far away as possible from the cutting end of the machine. It is also a good idea to use a power breaker so you don't electrocute yourself if you do slash through the power line. These can be bought in any hardware store; they divert the supply of electricity to the machine, so making it safer.

A few other points: remember that electric tools should never be used in wet conditions, and even if you are leaving it unattended only for a few minutes, always switch an electirc tool off at the mains. Finally, as with a petrol-powered machine, remember to turn it off before you clean it or examine it in any way.

Essential Tools	Useful Tools
• Spade	• Clippers
• Fork	• Secateurs
• Rake	• Edger
• Trowel	• Hoe
• Watering can	• Weed-grubber
• Bucket	• Axe

3. Soil Matters

Soil, the absolute essential for any sort of cultivation and growth, is a by-product of the earth's rocky base. The action of wind and rain and other upheavals over the millennia has helped grind the elemental rock into a pulp. This, combined with moisture and other organic matter, we call soil.

Soil differs from one area to another in the same way as water. One soil is rich in lime while another might be sandy. In some places, the stony origins of soil are still obvious, with lots of pebbles surfacing when you dig even a little below the surface.

The earth we dig into consists of three main layers. For gardeners, the top layer, extending to about 70cms (2ft) below the surface and called topsoil, is especially important. This is where most of our garden plants live, although their roots spread into a looser, more granulated layer below. Called the subsoil, this is about as deep as the topsoil, but stonier. Finally comes the lower layer, which taps into the ground water. From this, moisture rises. To make soil fertile, water is absolutely vital and, in well-drained soil, moisture passes up and down constantly through the three layers of earth.

Good soil is easy to recognise. It looks like the inside of a loaf of rough wholemeal bread – crumbly and evenly textured, with no big lumps or stones, and neither too wet nor too dry. Few of us are lucky enough to have soil so perfect and it can be

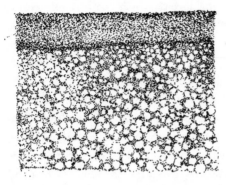

Cross-section of topsoil and subsoil

both frustrating and fascinating to see what a seemingly ordinary suburban garden can throw up with a bit of digging. Broken china, hair combs, rotting wood, bricks, the metal remains of a paintbrush, plastic bags, and bits of bicycle and pram, are nothing unusual.

Most soil can be redeemed and turned into a good growing medium, though if your house is on a new housing estate and your garden is covered in weeds and splattered with remnants of the builder's labour, it may be worth saving yourself months of back-breaking work, with no guarantee of any improvement, by buying in new topsoil.

For the rest of us, the task is simple enough. When you start out, dig up as much as you can of your flowerbeds, using a spade and a fork. The best times are late autumn, to kill off the remains of the season's weeds and leave the garden looking tidy for the winter, and then sometime in March when the temperature starts rising and the ground is not frozen solid. Avoid digging at any time when the soil is very wet.

Digging breaks up impacted clods of earth and refreshes the surface, which is probably covered with half-dead weeds and old grass, along with blown-in crisp bags and sweet wrappers. It also brings stones to the surface which can be collected for other uses, such as weighing down flowerpots. Clean up the soil as you go and take a couple of days if necessary: digging can be heavy work.

If the flowerbeds need serious resuscitation, there is the technique known as double digging, which will literally turn your garden upside down. You dig a trench about as deep as two spade lengths, putting the dug earth to one side and loosening the bottom of the trench with a fork. If you reach the orange subsoil, leave it alone. Next dig a new trench beside the first and turn the soil into the first, incorporating some compost, leaf-mould or manure as you go. And so on. When you come to the final trench, use the soil from the first trench to fill it up. This is heavy work, but once done, your bed will be easy to manage and will not need the same treatment for at least another five seasons, if ever. The bed will also be slightly raised, so you may like to contain it with bricks or a length of wood.

Acid or Alkaline?

All soils have a certain amount of nutrients, vital for healthy plants. But these nutrients do not last forever and must be replaced, as nothing will grow otherwise. In the past, this was one reason why farmers would leave an overworked field lie fallow for a couple of years.

So how do we do enrich our soil and keep it healthy? First, it is useful to know what kind of soil you have, and for this purpose, we need a little bit of chemistry.

Even in one garden, not all the soil will have the same properties. This is logical when you consider that not all soil is made up of the same ingredients. For example, if you live near the sea, you can expect more sand in your soil. The magic words used in most gardening manuals are 'acid', meaning sour and bog-like, and 'alkaline', meaning rich in lime. For little cost, you can buy kits that will help you determine exactly how acid (with a low pH) or alkaline (a high pH) your garden is. There is even a thermometer-like spike for sale that you can poke into different parts of the garden to get absolutely precise readings.

Soil pH Readings

7.3-8.0	Alkaline (rich in lime)	Hydrangea pink
7.0	Mid-point/normal	Hydrangea purple
5.5-6.5	Slightly acid	
4.5-6.5	Very acid	Hydrangea blue

The term pH is a measure of acidity and alkalinity, with pH 7.0 the mid-point; pure water measures 7. A reading of 4.5 to 5.5 means the soil is very acidic and ideal for rhododendrons, azaleas, camellias and most heathers. In a slightly acid soil, reading 5.5 to 6.5, most fruit trees and bushes will flourish, along with roses and lawn grass. Manure, chemical fertilizers and acid rain tend to make a soil acidic; if this happens, digging in some lime will cure the problem. Lime can be added to compost, but not to manure, as this will cause a release of ammonia gas, and nitrogen will be lost from the soil. Neutral soil, reading 6.5 to 7.3, is the ideal and almost anything will grow in it. Alkaline soil, rich in lime, is yellowish and reads from 7.3 to 8.0. Carnations, wallflowers and cabbages prefer it. Too much lime is not a good thing as it causes soil to break up quickly.

Initially at least, you may not need to go to the bother of fiddling around with soil samples and test-tubes. A simple examination of your garden will give you plenty of clues. For a start, identify the weeds that flourish in your lawn and flowerbeds. If you get lots of daisies and plantain in the lawn, and maybe even thistles and buttercups, then your soil is acidic, or low in lime. Clover, by contrast, prefers an alkaline soil. If nettles are flourishing, count yourself lucky: the soil is particularly fertile. If there are any hydrangeas in the garden or nearby, observe their colour in summer. The blooms will turn pink with lime soil, blue with acid or purple in neutral soil.

Picking up a handful of moist earth after scraping away the dry surface of your flowerbed can also tell a tale. If it looks and feels gritty and cannot be rolled into a ball, it is sandy and will require plenty of sticky compost (cow or pig manure) to turn it into a suitable base for growing. It will also need lots of watering. On a positive note, it is easy to dig.

On the opposite end of the scale is a heavy soil. This one makes a sausage-shape when rolled in the hand; if you rub it between the fingers, it turns shiny because it is rich in clay. Think of the ideal soil for mud pies and you've got it. Water moves very slowly through this type of soil, so it can get waterlogged in winter and dry out in summer. It may need some kind of artificial drainage, or, at the very least, double digging in the autumn. This is heavy work; I would consider getting in a professional gardener and possibly a mechanical digger if you have this problem.

Fortunately, most of us have soil that falls somewhere between these two extremes. Your average soil is a bit like a light plum pudding – rich, but not too rich, and easy enough to handle. Rubbed in the hand, its breaks up into medium-sized 'crumbs'. A good layer of rich compost in the autumn will keep it healthy.

Don't worry about your soil type too much. Most plants will grow in anything reasonable, dressed up with some good manure. The only ones I would avoid are the lime-haters that refuse to grow in an alkaline soil. Remember, the secret of good gardening is finding the plants that suit your particular conditions. With luck, this will be a rewarding search.

Earth to Earth

Humus is the dark brown mass of partially decomposed organic matter contained in all soil. Without it, soil would be sand. Humus is made up of the rotted remains of plants, insects and other dead things. Left long enough, everything disintegrates and is assimilated into the surrounding ground, adding to its richness and becoming a breeding ground for the next generation of plant and insect life. By encouraging growth and renewal, humus-rich soil is the foundation for all life, and we mess with it at our peril.

In the typically overused garden, the humus content of your soil can do with a little help and there are many soil improvers for sale. In my garden shed I keep a 5kg bag of multi-purpose compost, which the providers boast is free from chemical additives and enriched with seaweed. It can be used for seed, potting and planting out. Along with the seaweed, it contains fully composted cattle manure, sphagnum moss and sand. In any garden centre, you will find John Innes composts. Innes (1829-1904) left money in his will to found a school for training gardeners. His trustees established a research institute instead, and developed the John Innes soil-based seed and potting composts that exist to this day. The higher the number, the richer they are in fertilizer. So No. 1 is used for seedlings, No. 2 for potting on and No. 3 for plants like tomatoes and chrysanthemums. After using, throw into the compost heap.

Types of Manure
- Poultry – available as pellets. Can burn plants
- Horse – a mixture of half-rooted straw and urine
- Mushroom – often lime-rich
- Cow/sheep – fairly moist, so best dug in

Farmyard manure, widely available directly from farms in large quantities or in more manageable plastic packs from garden centres, is one of the best sources of nourishment for the soil. Chicken manure and mushroom compost are two varieties worth watching out for. Manure must be 'well-rotted' before use. This is because manure generates a lot of heat when breaking down, and if applied in this state, will damage a plant's roots.

Manure can be the gardener's best friend, although not quite as easy to find in suburbia as in the heart of the countryside. If possible, buy in bulk and be prepared to take delivery by the tonne – sharing with a few neighbours might be an idea. If the manure is fresh, leave it to cool down for about six weeks, with a plastic sheet over it as protection from the rain. Add some of it to the compost bin as an activator.

A good tonic for wilting plants is liquid manure. This is easily made. In a bucket, mix a shovel of manure with three times its volume in water. Stir it vigorously and pour on the plants.

Peat moss, organic, weed-free and easy to handle, is also widely available, but comes from a valuable and dwindling natural resource. When the bogs go, a precious eco-system, supporting numerous wild plants, insects and animals, will be lost forever. The good news is that sphagnum moss, a renewable resource, may work as an alternative, while experiments are also being carried out on shredded coconut shells. So think before you buy your next sack of peat moss.

Another alternative to peat moss is leaf-mould, the brown, flaky material that dead leaves turn into. To make your own, simply stack the rotting leaves in a wire-netting enclosure or put them in a black bin-bag, making a few holes in the sides of this and adding a special accelerator that is available in all garden centres. The best leaf-mould comes from oak or beech. Leave out pine needles, plane, sycamore, holly or other leathery evergreens, as they will take too long to rot. Leaf-mould is ideal for woodland plants, like trilliums and snowdrops. It can also be used in potting mixture for alpines (one-third leaf-mould to one-third compost and one-third grit). It can be crumbled up when rubbed between the hands or put through a coarse garden sieve. As a mulch, use it as it is.

Another essential for the gardener is bonemeal, a slow-acting fertilizer that is excellent for putting in the bottom of the planting hole in autumn and spring. It is particularly useful for bulbs, which are not generally partial to rich farmyard manure. Then there is sand or grit, essential for helping drainage. Horticultural sand only should be used. Grit consists of small chippings of stone and is invaluable for working into heavy soil. It is also used when making up composts for alpines and bulbs and when making a raised bed.

Digging

Once you have your supply of manure or compost, you can apply it by digging it in or by mulching. If you decide to dig, wait a few days after your initial digging and clearing before adding the compost and then make sure not to go deeper than about 20cms (8ins). Even if you have removed a lot of stones, the compost will add to the bulk of your soil, so after mixing it well in, use a rake to smooth over the surface.

Mulching

Not everyone thinks digging is necessary; at least not every year. Mulching is a less backbreaking way of enriching the soil and can help revive an overgrown bed. It involves spreading the compost over the soil surface and allowing it to sink in slowly. It is easier than digging, and because it lies on the surface, can have an insulating effect.

Mulching is ideally used around shrubs, trees and herbaceous borders. It keeps the soil moist and cool during hot summer days, promoting growth and keeping weeds in check. With the help of hard-working worms and other insects, the goodness in the mulch is gradually dragged through the soil. Compost is not the only material used for mulching. Shredded bark, leaf-mould and small pebbles or grit can be used. Some people use grass cuttings, but as these usually contain dormant seeds, it is not really a good idea unless you want grass to grow around your plants. Plastic mulches in the form of black sheets can also be used, and are especially useful under a gravel driveway or path. For flowerbeds, perforated sheets are available which let in air and water. But unlike organic cover-ups, plastic of any kind does the soil no good in the long term.

The best time of the year for mulching is May. First prepare the soil by cleaning it up, removing dead leaves, weeds and other rubbish, and giving everything a good watering if the warm weather has already set in. Sprinkle in a bit of fertilizer as well. Now spread a thin layer of your mulch under the branches and leaves, leaving the space directly around the stems clear. In the autumn, fork whatever remains of the mixture into the topsoil. Repeat the process the following spring. All mulches are attractive to snails and slugs, so be vigilant.

DIY Compost-making

Even the worst gardener knows that throwing your garden and kitchen waste on the herbaceous border in its raw state is not a good idea. But leave that waste to rot down into compost or humus and it can add greatly to your garden's general health.

Making your own compost is not at all hard; any heap of vegetation will eventually rot down. But, ideally, you need a confined space, such as a bin, to allow the refuse to generate heat and encourage bacteria. Air is also needed, as is water, though not too much – a waterlogged compost heap just won't work. So find a good spot in the garden, preferably dry and shaded. That dull corner that grows nothing but moss could be ideal. You can buy a compost container or tumbler; these are probably best for the average city garden and work well. Still, making your own with some bricks and bits of timber is not too hard and ensures that it fits exactly into your space. To do this, build a small brick or wooden bin, with four sides and a rainproof lid. Find a piece of old carpet to cover the compost. Ideally, one of the side panels should be in two sections so that the top half can be lifted off to make the compost more accessible. Even better, make two wooden containers and as the compost heap matures, turn it into the second container. This will leave the rotted compost on top and readily accessible. Also available in your local garden centre is a type of plastic fencing that can be made into a round compost bin for garden cuttings. So there are lots of options.

What to Put in Your Compost Bin

Start off with a layer of twigs to ensure that air can get to the bottom of the pile. Then into your bin throw your garden and kitchen waste: fruit and vegetable leftovers, tea-bags, eggshells, grass cuttings, hedge and other garden clippings, dead plants, shredded cardboard and paper, hair and wool. Seaweed, if you can get it, helps make excellent compost. To make the best use of your grass cuttings, don't use too much at a time and cover a layer of grass with cardboard and repeat as necessary. Even clothes made of natural fibres can be added to the heap, though it is best to cut them up first. Do not add meat, fish, bread, or indeed anything cooked or processed. These stink while rotting and attract rats. Deep-rooted perennial weeds are not a good idea for the compost heap while fresh, but once dried out, can be used. Otherwise, they are best burned.

It is important to get the mixture right – a layer of grass should be followed by a layer of kitchen refuse and a layer of manure or even garden soil to help speed up decay. This you will find happens naturally, but if you have too much of anything, leave it to one side in a bucket or make a second small heap. Remember to keep the mixture covered. If the compost gets too wet, add straw, sawdust or even hedge clippings. If it gets too dry, water it or add fresh grass clippings. You do not have to add to the compost heap every day. Keep a special bin for kitchen leftovers and tip them in once a week.

There is some argument about whether it is better to leave everything alone or to turn over the mixture occasionally. The compost heap must be allowed to ferment, so on the whole, leaving it to its own devices is probably better than messing with it too often. The biggest problem is getting at the rotted matter at the bottom, especially in plastic containers as the compost within gets very compacted and hard to dig out.

Patience is needed with a compost heap. It will take from three months to a year for everything to decompose fully. The smaller the ingredients, the quicker it will all rot, so cut up your vegetable remains clippings before adding them to the heap; think of it as making a soup. For the less patient among us, garden centres sell a compost accelerator. This acts like a yeast starter in bread- or wine-making. The traditional compost activator is urine, which has the virtue of being readily available, while chicken pellets are also good. When everything has decomposed, the compost should look like a very dark, crumbly, fibrous soil or humus. For those with sensitive noses, be reassured that proper compost has a lovely, rich smell and does not stink at all.

Fertilizers

Creating and maintaining a healthy soil is the fundamental principle of healthy gardening. If compost is the food, then fertilizers are the vitamin pills, and therefore not to be relied on all the time.

All plants need nitrogen, phosphates and potash, often sold together as NPK; the protein, fat and carbohydrates of the vegetable world. Nitrogen helps leaves to grow and promotes healthy green foliage. Phosphates are vital for healthy root development. Potash (another name for potassium) not only ensures better yields of flowers, fruits and vegetables, but also makes plants more drought- and disease-resistant. Other nutrients, such as magnesium, manganese and iron, are needed in smaller quantities, but are not as important.

Although chemical fertilizers can give a plant a big initial boost, they ultimately create soft, weak plants that are prey to pests and disease. Nor are they good for the soil, poisoning worms, bacteria and fungi, three elements vital for keeping soil healthy. Because of their solubility, fertilizers can find their way into the ground water, so polluting rivers, lakes and even the sea to disastrous effect, as has been found in farming areas all over the world.

By the standards of artificial fertilizers, the amounts of available nitrogen, potassium and phosphorus from organic matter – that is, matter that was once alive – is low. It still contains everything that the garden needs in a natural form.

For the growth-promoting properties of nitrogen, use anything rich in protein, such as blood, fish and bone meal and even diluted urine. Bone meal is also a source of phosphorus and potassium, while seaweed is rich in potassium and trace elements, as is rock potash. Wood ash is the traditional source of potash. As the hazards of using chemical fertilizers have become better known, garden centres are stocking up on natural alternatives, so they are readily available.

Preparing the Soil

To prepare a new bed for flowers or vegetables, spread well-rotted farmyard manure over the soil and then fork it in. Leave for a few days to settle before planting. With established plants, spread manure around their roots as mulch. Do this at least twice a year – in autumn to give the soil a winter overcoat and in spring to prepare for the forthcoming season's growth.

Compost-Heap Recipe

- Broken up branches (on the bottom)
- Kitchen waste
- Grass cuttings, annual weeds and garden clippings
- Manure or soil
- Shredded newspaper
- Wood or peat ashes (not coal)
- Seaweed

DO NOT include:
- Meat
- Fish
- Bread
- Cooked leftovers
- Perennial weeds, like dandelions

4. From Little Seeds

Sooner or later, you are going to be tempted by those collections of colourful seed packets on sale every spring. Growing from seed seems a nice idea but it can be frustrating as not every seed is guaranteed to grow into a thick bush or dazzling bloom and, sometimes, an entire packet can fail to germinate. On a positive note, this is unusual and it is fascinating to see how seemingly identical seeds, sown together, can grow at vastly differing speeds. Some of these are soon strong enough for transplanting, while others grow too fast, developing weak, thin stems, and then fall over and die.

The time to think of growing from seed is in early spring; the ideal time will be given on the back of the seed packet. If the weather is still chilly, there is no point in rushing – seeds planted when the weather is warmer will catch up quickly and are often less prone to disease than those put down earlier. With better light, they are also less likely to grow too fast. Initially at least, avoid seeds that need special treatments, such as chilling, to force germination, or difficult plants like begonia which need the expert touch if they are to flourish.

Before you start, you need a seed tray, some pots, compost and a covering. All kinds of good value seed trays are now available and they are a neat way of bringing on a number of seeds at once. Specialised seed propagators are widely available but not really necessary. The kitchen can provide all sorts of containers, like yoghurt and butter tubs. All they need is a good cleaning and then a few holes pierced in the base for drainage.

Fill the seed tray or pot with compost and then press this down, so that the surface is even. Water carefully and allow to drain. Add a little more compost to make a bed for the seeds. Shake your seeds carefully from the packet on to this surface. A good method of ensuring that you get a straight line of seeds is by folding a sheet of paper in half to make a simple funnel. Put the seeds in the fold and see how much easier it is to control them as they drop into the seed tray. Small seeds do not need a covering of compost. For bigger ones, make a hole in the compost with a pencil, a fork handle, or a special implement called a dibber or dibble, and drop in the seed.

Cover with more compost or even better, with a substance called vermiculite that, unlike compost, lets the light in but also holds moisture. It can be bought in most garden centres. To protect seeds from direct sunlight, spread a sheet of newspaper over the seed tray. If your seeds need darkness to sprout, put the pot or seed tray in a dark plastic bag or wrap them in kitchen foil. Label everything carefully, and then place somewhere warm, though not in direct sunlight. The airing cupboard is ideal.

Depending on the plant, you should see the first evidence of germination within a week. These first leaves, called seed leaves, are like a child's baby teeth and are not the true leaves of the plant. As soon as the seedlings sprout, bring them into the light and make sure the compost stays moist. If you leave them too long in the dark, they will develop long, spindly stems as they stretch upwards to seek the light. Be careful when watering, as it is all too easy to wash the seedlings away; it is better to use a mister. When the seedlings sprout their first 'true' leaves and are large enough to handle, move the better examples into pots, using an ordinary kitchen fork to lever them out of the seed tray and taking care not to damage the fragile roots and stem. At the same time, be ruthless and throw out the weaklings. This stage is called 'pricking out'.

Always hold the seedlings by the small seed leaves to avoid damaging the stem. Have your pot ready with fresh, moist compost, make a small hole in it with a fork handle or pencil and then ease the seedling's roots into the hole. Still holding the seedling by the leaf, gently push the compost over the roots. Pots can be placed on the kitchen windowsill, where it is easy to keep an eye on them, but must be protected from the burning effect of strong sunlight. Even at this stage, you will see that some seedlings progress at a faster rate than others. Water them regularly and carefully. All going well, the stems develop hairs and more leaves start appearing. They are entering the adolescent phase of their development.

When the time comes to plant them outdoors, take it in stages. Leave the plants outside during the day, but bring them back indoors at night for about a week; this is called 'hardening off'. Next leave them outdoors all the time, but cover the seedlings with plastic mineral water bottles cut in half. These will protect them from the worst of the elements. If more ambitious, acquire or build your own cold frame, a small wooden or concrete frame with a glass lid that can fit several flowerpots, and will help the plants make the transition from the controlled climate indoors to the more unpredictable conditions waiting outside the back door.

Next step is to put the plants in the ground. Make sure the soil is ready by giving it a good digging a few weeks earlier, removing all weeds, stones and lumps. Seedlings do not like thick, lumpy earth. So before planting, rake the ground flat

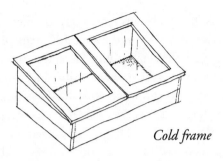

Cold frame

and then firm it down by walking on it. Rake it again, adding some fine compost. Dig a hole at least as deep as the pot currently holding the young plant, and after removing the plant from its pot, place it carefully in the ground, leaving plenty of space for the roots. Fill up the hole, making sure that the stem of the plant is at ground level. Press down firmly around the plant with your knuckles to remove any air pockets. Water well and check it every day for the first week at least. It is also worth feeding young plants once a week with one of the many organic fertilizers on sale everywhere, which can easily be added to the watering can.

Many seeds, such as lettuce, can be planted directly outdoors. Prepare the seedbed as above, by digging it well, removing all weeds, stones and other rubbish, then raking it smooth and adding some manure or compost. Into this crumbly tilth, or surface layer, make a narrow groove for your seeds, using the handle of your trowel, or the edge of a hoe or rake. It is better not to sow directly from the packet. Shake a few seeds into the palm of your hand and pinch out the seeds individually, or use the paper funnel method. Always sow more than you think you will need, since not all the seeds will germinate. Cover with a shallow layer of soil or compost and do not water.

As soon as the first shoots appear, protect them from birds, slugs and other pests. When the seed drill starts to get a little crowded, separate the small plants out so that they have room to spread. This tedious job, known as thinning, will ensure that each plant gets enough space and will help determine the eventual size of the plant and its yield if it is a vegetable. Throw out any of the weaker seedlings. For advice on spacing for individual plants, read the instructions on the seed packet. In the first thinning, the plants can be about twice as close as when they are fully grown. As soon as they start crowding each other, thin again.

Few gardeners will use up an entire packet of seeds at one time. So what to do with the leftovers? Like all natural products, seeds do not last forever. When bought, they will be contained in a sealed airtight packet, keeping them fresh. To preserve remaining seeds, close the packet tightly and either seal in a plastic bag or in a screw-top jar before storing in a cool, dark place. I wrap mine in plastic and keep them in used film containers, which are small and easy to label.

Cuttings

If you have even a small interest in your garden, you will find it hard to resist the trays of plants prominently displayed in every shopping centre. They are cheap and cheerful, you tell yourself. But add up the cost of those impulse buys over a year and you could give yourself a shock.

In the days before garden centres and shopping malls, gardeners increased their stock by taking cuttings from existing plants (either their own or those of friends and neighbours) towards the end of the growing season. This is still a cheap and satisfying way of making your garden grow.

Softwood cutting

Softwood cutting with heel

Like growing from seed, you probably won't get it right the first time. It is best to start with a softwood perennial that is easy to replicate, such as lavender or fuchsia. To take a cutting, just snip a few young shoots that haven't flowered, about 10cms (4ins) long, from the main plant, cutting them off just below a leaf joint, or with a 'heel' of the main stem still attached. Strip off all the leaves except the top two, so that you have a clean piece of shoot about 5cms (2ins) long. Fill a medium-sized flowerpot (7.5cms/3ins) with compost and water it. Make a number of small holes in the compost with a pencil, a stick or a kitchen fork handle and stick in your cuttings, making sure that the remaining leaves are kept well clear of the surface. If you wish, you can dip the stems in a special hormone-rooting powder that helps new roots to grow and stops the stems rotting. Firm gently around each cutting with your fingers. Stick the pot in a plastic bag and seal it. If the shoots are quite high, use bits of cane stuck in the pot to keep the polythene off the top leaves. Then put the pot somewhere out of direct sunlight and wait. The cutting will form a callous over the cut stem and it is from this that the new roots form.

Not all the cuttings will take, but after a couple of weeks, it should be obvious that some of them are developing new leaves. At this point removed the plastic covering. Resist the temptation to lift the shoots to see if they have developed roots, but give them a gentle tug. If they have not taken, they will lift out of the pot.

Next comes the nail-biting time. You just place the shoots somewhere cool and hope that they continue to flourish. As this is often an end-of-season job, you will not be sure how successful you have been until the following spring. Leave the new plants alone and water them only if they look parched. It is all to easy to drown a plant in winter when, like many animals, they are in a state of half-hibernation and just want to be left alone. Among the plants that can be propagated in this way are such garden standards as camellia, cotoneaster, forsythia, fuchsia and hydrangea.

Taking hardwood cuttings from trees and shrubs in the autumn is an even easier option. Although these take longer to

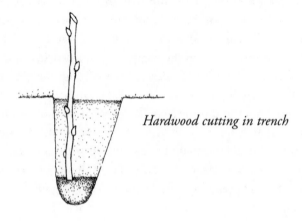

Hardwood cutting in trench

root, they don't need heat, and so can be planted outdoors. Choose a fresh but sturdy-looking shoot about 40cms (1ft 4 ins) in length. Chop off the top just above a bud and the bottom just below a bud, leaving you with about 30cms (1ft) of shoot. Dip the bottom into a growth-promoting hormone. Dig a trench and place some sand on the bottom to prevent water-logging around the cuttings. Stick in the cutting, leaving about a third of it above the ground. If you have a few to plant, leave about 15cms (6ins) between them. Replace the soil carefully, firming it down as you go to eliminate any pockets of air that would cause the cuttings to dry out, and, when completely filled, water thoroughly. Shrubs and trees that can be propagated in this way include forsythia, dogwood, poplar, plane, willow and vibunum, as well as most species of roses.

Leaf Cuttings

This form of propagation truly is miraculous. You cut a leaf from a plant, using a sharp knife. Put the leaf on a hard surface with the underside facing up and cut out the long mid-rib. Fill a tray with compost, water it well, and make two shallow trenches using a kitchen fork handle or dibber. Insert the two cut halves of the leaf into these trenches. Put inside a clear plastic bag, seal it so that no air gets in and place it somewhere out of direct sunlight. Young shoots will grow along the edges of the cut leaf edges.

Division

As well as being vital for the continued health of your perennials, division is the quick and easy way of increasing your stock of pot-plant favourites, especially ferns. Before doing anything, make sure the pot is well-soaked with water. Remove the plant carefully and lay it on some newspaper. With your hands, gently tease the plant apart, exposing some of the roots. If this isn't possible, use a hand fork or pair of secateurs to cut through the root ball. Don't worry – this won't harm the roots if done when the flowering season is over, or in early spring before growth has begun again. Ensure that each new plant has a strong shoot and healthy root system and cut off any over-long roots. Prepare a few pots with compost, preferably the same variety used in the original pot, and water well. Place the divided plants into the pots and water well. Keep out of direct sunlight to allow new roots to develop.

Growing from Layering

Layering is a propagation method used with shrubs like camellia or magnolia, climbers like clematis and fruits like the common blackberry. Take a shoot that can be bent down to the ground. Make a slanting cut halfway through the stem with a sharp knife. Fix the stem with the cut facing downwards into the ground with a bent piece of wire or a hair clip and place a stone on top. Keep well watered all summer to ensure rooting. You should be able to cut it free for replanting in the autumn.

Some plants, such as phygelius and winter jasmine, layer by themselves. A low-growing branch resting on the soil will take root. Gently dig up the rooted portion, snip it free from the parent plant with a pair of secateurs and put it in a pot of compost, or elsewhere in the garden. Water well.

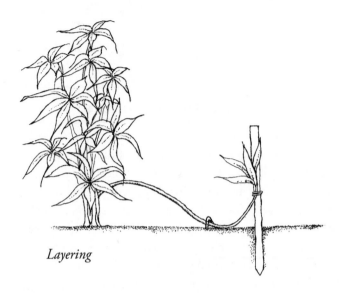

Layering

Top Tips on Planting from Seed

◆ Keep empty mineral water containers to use
as mini cloches

◆ Prepare all soil well before planting
anything

◆ Label all seedlings and cuttings

◆ Use glass jars and discarded film containers
to keep seeds fresh

◆ Take cuttings in spring and autumn

◆ Divide perennials and pot plants in spring

5. Nurturing Nature

Once the plant has been brought home from the garden centre and is safely in the ground, you may think that your work is over. In fact, it is just beginning. Especially in their first season, plants need lots of watering and feeding. The soil around their roots must be kept clear of weeds that could inhibit healthy growth and, in winter, they may require protection from frost.

It doesn't end there. As the months pass and plants grow bigger, you may decide to move them. Hedges need trimming and roses require pruning. Climbers must be staked. Unruly specimens in the herbaceous border should be lifted and divided. Fortunately, none of these jobs take too long. The no-maintenance garden may not exist, but a few minutes a day can be enough to keep your garden trouble-free.

Watering

Even a novice gardener knows that plants require watering. This is the one lesson we have all learned. The problem is that there is more to watering than pouring fluid into a flowerbed. There is a time to water and a time to leave your plants alone. Otherwise they die.

In winter, for instance, plants, like animals, are hibernating and don't need much watering. You may have brought some precious container plant indoors to protect it from the worst of winter. Because it is convenient, the temptation will be to tend it most carefully, giving it a little drink every time you see it. As it starts to wilt, you will water it even more and wonder why it is now draped over the edge of the pot. The answer is simple: you have drowned the poor thing.

In summer, by contrast, plants can't survive without water, as you will find out if you go away on holiday and neglect to get a plant sitter. We all know the effect drought has on growth and with summers getting warmer, it is vital to water all plants every day at least once, even when it appears to be raining all the time. Particularly at risk are all the new plants you put down in the spring, both flowers and vegetables, as their roots are not well established enough to find water for themselves. Climbers are also at risk, while any plant weakened by thirst is more vulnerable to pests such as the aphid, which, in a healthy state, it would shrug off. Sometimes you may think a plant is in good health despite your seeming neglect but the following year you will find that it does not flower as well as you might have hoped.

All soil has a reserve of moisture. It still needs at least two centimetres (about an inch) of rain per week in summer and a centimetre in spring and autumn if it is not to dry out. This will be particularly obvious with a lawn and so, before watering a dry lawn, use a garden fork to spike the soil, so that the water won't run off the top.

Watering should begin before plants start to show signs of wilting, in the same way as humans need fluid long before they feel thirsty. If your plants have already started wilting, it is too late. In a big garden, with a mixture of lawn and plants, you will need a hose and possibly a sprinkler system. Repeated trips back to the tap with your watering can will pall pretty quickly.

Start by planning the garden with some care. Plants that

need shade, for instance, should not be planted in a spot which gets the sun all day long. For these 'hot spots', pick plants from dry areas like the Mediterranean which are bred to thrive in constant heat. Good sense also suggests that you put plants that need lots of watering in the same area. Careful watering will help plants spread their roots to find their own supply of moisture in times of drought. To encourage this habit, aim the can or hose at the base of the plant. Sprinkling water on the foliage is worse than nothing as it encourages the roots to grow too close to the soil's surface.

Be careful not to water too strongly as a blast of water aimed at the plant's base could wash soil away from the roots. For a gentler spray of water, turn the rose at the end of the watering can spout upwards. Ideally, you should water in the evening when there is less chance of the water evaporating. If you water in strong sunshine, the drops can act as lenses and may cause foliage to scorch. Under glass, seedlings and young plants will require close attention, as a sunny day, even if cold outside, could kill them all.

Plants in containers require watering twice a day in hot conditions. At other times of the year, you may think they are getting plenty of rain water, but spring and autumn winds can dry them out. Check them every week and soak if necessary, except in frosty conditions. In winter, growth is at a standstill and plants do not absorb water. An over-watered plant looks limp and dejected, its pot is too heavy and the soil is cold and sodden. Over-watering will also encourage grey mould.

A drought is defined as a continuous period of fifteen days without rain. In such conditions, when restrictions on garden watering are put in place, there is still plenty you can do to keep your garden growing. Remove container plants from sunny spots into the shade. When you mow the lawn, leave the clippings where they lie to act as a mulch. It is important not to disturb the soil, particularly when weeding, so it might be worth just cutting the weeds off at soil level. Compost and mulch applied to the base of a plant can help soil retain water, particularly when mixed with water-retaining granules.

It might be worth considering recycling water. Certainly it is easy enough to install a water barrel to collect rain coming from the gutters, keeping it free of algae by giving it an occasional scrubbing. Providing the family does not use too much shower gels and shampoo, it is also possible to recycle bathroom water. Ask a friendly, conservation-minded plumber for further advice.

Planting

Most of your plants will come in pots from the garden centre. To give them the best possible start in your garden, first soak the lot – plant and pot – in a bucket of water for at least thirty minutes. Now dig a hole in the ground that is at least as big as the pot. In the bottom, mix in some compost and maybe a pinch or two of bone meal or another slow-acting fertilizer. Remove the plant carefully from the pot, with one hand firmly around the base of the plant, and check the root system. If it looks like one big tangle, ease some of the roots out carefully. Place the plant in the ground gently, taking care not to damage the roots, and fill the hole. Unless told otherwise by the label, make sure that the plant is not sitting higher than the surrounding ground. Firm down the soil around the plant to prevent air pockets developing. Water well and continue to water every day until the plant is firmly established, with new foliage or flowers developing. This will take at least a week with smaller plants and much longer with tree and shrubs.

Moving Shrubs

As a novice gardener, you probably will not get your garden arrangements right first time and so the temptation to move your shrubs and perennials could prove irresistible, either because you feel a certain plant would do better in a different location, or simply because you don't like it where it is.

Perennials are easy to move, as are small shrubs before their roots have become too established. Move plants in autumn or early spring when they are not growing. Make sure the ground is not too hard or waterlogged and wait until late in the day. Water the ground well for a few days before. At the same time, decide where you are going to place the uprooted plant and prepare the ground thoroughly so that the transfer can be made as quickly as possible. Now get the plant ready by tying back its foliage and stems with garden string. This should help make the digging easier. Start digging in a circle around the plant's roots. Here the process becomes a little hit and miss. Use a fork at first and dig it in under the plant. Lever it upwards and see if you can move it easily. If not, dig wider and deeper, using a spade, before trying again; it is important to move as much of the root system as possible. Ease the plant free of the ground and lift into a wheelbarrow, bucket or plastic bag to carry it to its new location.

After it has been transplanted, put a covering of mulch on the ground around the stem and keep an eye on it for at least a fortnight. Larger trees and shrubs can also be moved, but this backbreaking work is better left to the professionals.

Thinning Out Borders

It is very easy to put too many young shrubs in a border,

forgetting just how high and wide they will grow. A plant like the grey-leafed senecio will grow twice as fast as other bushes and should be pruned back hard before it becomes a complete nuisance (for information on pruning, see page 56). When I finally got around to tackling one of mine, I found a fuchsia underneath!

An out-of-control perennial is easier to tackle and can be divided to provide extra plants for another part of the garden or for a friend. To divide a perennial, lift it up with a large fork on as cool a day as possible, preferably in autumn or spring. The natural division points should be obvious, so split the plant by hand, ensuring that each section has its own root. Replant divided sections immediately in some other section of the garden or in a pot, trimming off old or large leaves carefully. If the plant has developed a clump of tough fibrous roots, the job may take two people. Drive two forks, or a fork and spade, into the roots, back to back, and then lever the plant apart. You will certainly do some damage but enough new growth should be salvaged to make the attempt worthwhile.

Supporting Climbers

Some climbers, like ivy or virginia creeper, have little suction pads on the ends of their leaves or tendrils that allow them to stick to concrete, wood or brick. Others, like clematis and honeysuckle, need trellis or wires to keep them in place. If the support is not attached properly to the wall or fence, a thriving honeysuckle is quite capable of pulling it down.

Attach wire netting to a wooden fence or the side of a garden hut with galvanised U-shaped staples that will hold the netting slightly away from the fence, giving the plant space to grow. For more vigorous climbers, use a system of horizontal

Vine eye screw

lines of wire. First buy some vine eye screws and galvanised wire at any DIY store. Screw a vine eye into the fence, put one end of a length of wire through one of its 'eyes' and make this secure by winding it back on itself. Put in another vine eye a metre or so distant and repeat, pulling the wire line until tight. On a wall, drill a hole in the wall, insert a plastic wall plug and then screw the vine eye in securely. Without damaging the stem, tie the plants to the wiring with garden twine. When planting, leave space so that air can circulate behind the climber by picking a spot about 20cms (8ins) out from the wall or support. This means the climber has to grow towards its support. You can use a cane to guide the young shoots in the right direction. When they reach the wall, twine a few of the larger stems to the wire lines and the plant will do the rest. If you have a panel fence, special plastic clips, available in garden centres, are quite effective.

It is possible to fix a trellis to a wall, but this requires attaching battens to the wall and then nailing the trellis into these. You may think this sounds like hard work, but drilling holes in a garden wall is a good way of refining your picture-hanging skills. However, I would advise sticking to the wire system, which is easy and cheap. As for a wooden fence, this must be strong enough to support its own weight, plus the trellis, and anything growing on it, even in a high wind.

Staking

Young trees need staking. Buy a stake about 1.5m (5ft) long and drive it into the ground to a depth of at least 60cms (2ft). Leaving the stake on the windward side, attach the sapling with two belt-style tree ties made from plastic or heavy webbing, one at ground level, the other where the branches begin. Tighten the ties on the stake, not on the growing tree, to minimise damage to the trunk. As the tree grows, make sure the ties have not become too tight. Old bicycle tubes make good ties.

Some perennials, removed from their natural habitat where they would lean up against other plants, need support. Canes are normally used, although elaborate metal and plastic frameworks, specially designed for plants like geraniums and peonies, can be bought. If you are using a cane, stick it securely in the ground beside the plant to a depth of about 25cms (10ins) and see that it stops about 15cms (6ins) below the height of the plant. Tie the plant to the stake with garden twine, taking care not to damage the stem.

For 'wigwam' supports, used in growing sweet peas, take between three and six canes and stick them in the ground in a circle. Lean them into each other and, at the top, tie securely, using rubber bands first and then garden twine.

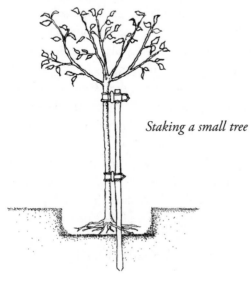

Staking a small tree

Pruning

Pruning is simply the removal of unwanted parts of a plant or hedge, though to the outsider it may seem like a difficult or delicate task. Take off too much and the plant dies. Take off too little and soon everything is out of control. Then there are roses, perhaps the most difficult and delicate of all plants when it comes to pruning. Yet go to a garden centre in late winter and you will see rose plants pruned right back, ready to grow even stronger the next year.

Clearly there is a technique to pruning. To end any fears of the task, try clipping a hedge. Take, for instance, the ubiquitous griselinia, beloved of new home-owners as a quick-growing screen. Clip this all you will and it will still grow back, defiantly bland and apple green. While you might wish you had killed it off, at least this experiment will have given you confidence and you will have found that pruning can indeed promote continued growth and improve a plant's general health.

In a plant with disease problems, pruning will involve snipping off everything that is dead, diseased or weak at any time of the year. In an established healthy plant, the tip of every stem will be growing vigorously and along its length you will see either new stems or tiny buds emerging. Cut back to just above one of these and it will spring into life, thanks to the light and space it is now getting. This light pruning, best done in spring, need hold no fear for anyone, even a total beginner, and ensures healthy bush-like growth. Just make sure your secateurs or clippers are clean and sharp and then choose a spot just above an outward-facing bud. Make a clean cut at a 45-degree angle, so that the lowest point of the cut is even with the top of the bud.

This also holds for small, soft plants, where the technique

of 'pinching out', or removing the soft shooting tips of young plants by hand, will make a plant grow outwards into an attractive bush rather than straggling upwards. Pinch out back to the next set of leaves.

Pruning something larger, such as a young fruit tree, is more complicated. Examine it from all angles before you start and imagine what it could look like in years to come if left unchecked. Decide what you want to take off. The easy decisions concern branches that are crossing and rubbing against main branches; they simply have to go. When in doubt, do nothing; once a branch is chopped off; it is gone forever and you may find that you have ruined your tree. This is definitely a job where expert advice is useful.

It is important to pick the right time of year for pruning. Hedges, both formal and informal, can be clipped at any time, but other plants are fussier, though you are safe enough if you stick to autumn or early spring, when nothing much is growing. With early-flowering shrubs, cut back all the branches that have bloomed after flowering. With plants that continue to bloom until later, get to work on cutting out weak, old and awkward shoots before the following spring when the whole cycle begins again.

If you are a rose fan, but hate the thorns and the pruning, here is some good news: meticulous pruning may not be necessary. There is plenty of evidence that cutting hybrid tea (large-flowered) and floribunda (cluster-flowered) types roughly with a secateurs or even a hedge trimmer will not do them any harm. Traditionally, hybrid tea roses are pruned right back to about two buds from the ground. The principles remain the same: you cut out all weak shoots and shorten strong stems to encourage new growth. Don't forget to wear thick garden gloves before doing any work on a rose bush.

Buddleias are the other plant that even the novice gardener will have to tackle. If you miss out on pruning them for a season or so, the stems will become too thick to cut with secateurs. So, in spring, cut the previous year's shoots back to between 2.5 and 5cms (1-2ins) from the ground. The result will be strong, tall shoots with lots of flowers. Left alone, the bush will still flower, but earlier and not as enthusiastically.

Other plants that can be pruned hard (the technical expression is 'stooled', meaning cut back to just above ground level) include dogwoods (*cornus*), ornamental brambles (*rubus*), willows (*salix*), eucalyptus and deciduous ceanothus.

Protecting Your Plants

Young plants may need protection from frost, snow and wind in winter. With small or newly planted shrubs, make a customised windbreak by sticking a few small canes in the ground around them and then wrapping plastic, cardboard or netting around these. A large plastic bag placed over the plant and pegged securely into the ground is another option when bad weather is forecast. Leave this on only for as long as is necessary. Larger shrubs on walls can be protected using special garden fleece, or the cut branches from conifers pushed into the soil in front of them as an improvised shield. The Christmas tree may well provide you with a few good branches. Small alpines, used to dry, cold conditions, may not flourish if they get waterlogged. Put a little roof over them, using a sheet of glass or rigid plastic supported on bricks.

As for snow, do your conifers a favour by knocking off heavy falls as soon as possible as the weight can damage the branches. Or, by winding a piece of twine around the outside of the tree's branches, simply tie the branches in to the tree before the snow comes to avoid this problem altogether.

Weeding

Ask any gardener their least favourite task and weeding is sure to come out on top. This is the job that never goes away, from early spring to late autumn and often right up to Christmas.

Left to their own devices, weeds will reclaim your garden at the expense of plants you have carefully nurtured for years. It can happen very quickly, as anyone who likes to take his or her holidays in mid-summer will tell you. A fortnight away in early July and the garden is almost unrecognisable when you come home.

Every garden will have its own collection of annual and perennial weeds. The good news is that in an established garden, from which most perennial weeds have long since been banished, a few minutes every day spent weeding by hand will ensure that nothing gets too well-established, even monsters, such as dandelions with their huge roots.

Bindweed. This fast-spreading weed entwines itself around garden plants.

Many people put gravel or bark mulch in their borders to help cut down on the weeding. In my garden, the weeds come up through anything and that includes bark mulch, which, as the birds love flinging it around, has added to my labours, not reduced them. Face it: if you have a garden, you're going to have to weed it regularly.

59

Easy Maintenance Tips

- ♦ Water every evening
- ♦ Weed little and often
- ♦ Prune in spring and autumn
- ♦ Mulch

6. The Garden Pest

Even those of us living in cities battle with nature every day of our lives. Watch your garden for any length of time and you will be stricken with a sense of your own insignificance. The earth belongs to a variety of birds, beasts, insects and amoeba that we can distract and occasionally chase away but will never conquer. For instance, I may have bought my house and garden, but the true owners are a family of magpies living in my next-door neighbour's tree. Any other bird that appears is swiftly chased away.

Another sobering sight is the compost box on a warm day. Open the lid to throw in the leftovers and you get a grandstand view of the lower stages of evolution. It is quite humbling. Dust we are and dust we certainly all become thanks to the hard work of thousands of energetic maggots that come to life through some miracle that I, for one, cannot claim to fully understand.

All this is by way of introducing the single most frustrating aspect of growing anything, and that is the daily war against slugs, aphids, flies, wasps, birds, ants, maggots and a range of animals from mice and rats to the urban fox and the friendly next-door mutt.

Weeds you can deal with; you pull them out and they may come back, but if you work hard enough, you will get results. But who has not felt a surge of anger at the sight of a row of small lettuce that appeared healthy and full of promise the day before and is now nothing more that a series of efficiently stripped stalks? Or at the holes drilled overnight into the leaves of a favourite flower or plant? Or the maggots that have eaten their way into your strawberries or blackcurrants? Or the slimy turd dumped by a phantom dog who has turned your front lawn into his personal toilet?

Garden centres must make a fortune from the bewildering range of powders, potions and mixes crowding their shelves as we attempt to kill off everything in our gardens except the plants. As well as powders to get rid of ants, there are the massive containers of slug pellets and, every year, new and original methods of discouraging domestic pets from wreaking havoc on the lawn, the flowerbeds and vulnerable trees. Even the most organic gardener must be tempted to succumb.

If you are reluctant to wage chemical warfare on your garden, there are ways of side-stepping trouble before it begins. Most of it is common sense. For a start, you should prepare your soil thoroughly before planting and remove all traces of weeds. Only then add in your manure, compost or other treatments. Healthy plants in good soil are less likely to fall prey to pests.

When sowing, use good-quality bulbs, seeds and cuttings. Throw out old seeds. Be ruthless when it comes to getting rid of any ailing plants or bringing poor quality plants into your garden, even if they did seem like a bargain down at the supermarket. Sow and plant properly, leaving no air pockets around the roots of new plants so that they can settle down as quickly as possible. Do the right jobs at the right time. Water and feed plants regularly, as a weak plant will attract all sorts of problems.

Prune your shrubs and trees diligently, cutting out dead

wood and thinning overcrowded branches. Buy a length of netting at your local garden centre, plus a selection of different-sized stakes and canes, and use these to guard seedlings, vegetables and soft fruit from birds. A cylinder of wire netting around the base of a tree will keep dogs away from the roots. Keep your garden tidy. Old boxes, rotting leaves and abandoned flowerpots are a breeding ground for slugs and woodlice.

Even if you are infested, there is still a lot that you can do without becoming too reliant on the chemical industry. Insects such as caterpillars can be removed by hand, and the flowerbeds kept clear of dead or mouldy leaves where pests can hide. Use the organic trick of 'companion planting'; for example, sowing a row of onions beside your carrots to help keep off carrot fly as this insect does not like the onion smell. Group a mixture of plants together so pests can't find their host plants easily. Try and attract 'good' insects into your garden. Hoverflies, for instance, that like to feast on aphids, are attracted by marigolds. Find out about other organic tricks from organisations such as the Henry Doubleday Research Foundation, whose website address is at the back of this book.

But first let us look over the past few decades when gardeners began taking pesticides for granted as a miracle cure. These work in various ways. They can kill the insect or its source of food. Or they can enter the plant and, as well as killing off any insects already installed, prevent further infestation; these are called 'systemic' herbicides. Then there are fungicides, used to control fungal diseases and sprayed on before the disease has taken hold. If you must use pesticides, wear a pair of rubber gloves to protect your hands. But if you accept that these substances harm your skin, just think what they can do to the rest of your body and to the environment generally. Think organic and try to use biodegradable 'botanical insecticides', such as pyrethrum, derris and insecticidal soap, which are available at your local garden centre.

Not all insects are pests. The worm, for instance, plays a vital role in aerating the soil, while bees spread pollen. Here is a short guide to pests you do not want around your garden, although aphids, slugs and caterpillars will certainly top everyone's hate list:

ANTS: It can be fascinating to watch a colony of ants at work as they carry a crumb of bread or a piece of grass back to their anthill. But it is their very industry that makes ants dangerous. They can loosen the soil around the roots of a plant, causing it to wilt and perhaps die. They can also carry greenfly from one plant to another.

APHIDS (Greenfly, blackfly): You can recognise these as a swarm of tiny flies, sucking the sap of plants, flowers and fruit trees, most notoriously roses and apples, breeding by the minute and then sending off their young to wreak further destruction. The vampires of the insect world, they also produce a sticky goo called honeydew that turns plants black. There are 80 varieties of aphid. If flicking them off by hand is impossible, hose them down with soapy water, or try using a vacuum cleaner. The ladybird is an aphid-eater, so be very happy if you spot one in your flowerbed.

BEETLES: Strawberries and raspberries can be eaten away by beetles. Control weeds and keep the area under the plants free of dead leaves and other debris, where the beetles can hide.

BIRDS: Birds can be a complete nuisance, especially in the early spring. Not only will they peck away at anything you have planted, they will toss aside carefully laid mulches and dressing to do so. They also like playing games with slug traps and get especially noisy if these are filled with beer, as I know from my family of alcoholic magpies. Protect seedlings and plants with fine-mesh wiring, using stakes and canes as support, and making a canopy at least beak-height above the plants. Birds also like flower buds and fruit such as plums. Netting is the only answer. As for seeds, few are safe from the tough beaks of the sparrow which can dig them out from under layers of compost or through the finest of netting. The only answer is to plant your seeds indoors and then protect seedlings under cut-offs from mineral water bottles. Bird-scaring devices can also be bought or improvised. Tear a black bin bag into strips and tie these to a stake, or lay lengths of old hose pipe under fruit trees; the birds think these are snakes.

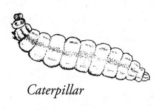

Caterpillar

CATERPILLARS: These butterflies and moths-to-be come in many varieties, some eating flower buds, others leaves, while the cutworm will attack plants at ground level, especially in late summer. Try to stop the butterfly landing and laying its eggs by putting a fine-netting mesh over precious plants; flick them off plants if you see them.

CHILDREN: Although children are not strictly classifiable as pests, it is one of the immutable laws of modern life that they play football wherever they can. Football and flower gardens do not go together. Other sports involve hitting smaller balls with a variety of bats and racquets, and swatting nearby flowers can quickly become part of the game. The damage may be limited by giving children a patch of their own where they can grow a few radish and nasturtium. With luck, this will give them some idea of the care needed to create a garden and a life-long love for growing things. To encourage junior gardeners, special packets of seeds for children are available, as are child-sized rakes and spades.

EARWIGS: These have their uses as they feed on aphids, but will eat flowers and leaves, with chrysanthemums and dahlias particular favourites. Smear grease on the stems of vulnerable plants to keep them away.

EELWORM: These can destroy a potato crop, particularly in new ground. An old cure is to rub the seed potatoes with lime before planting. It is also worth selecting a variety, such as Pentland Javelin, which is resistant to some types of this pest.

LEATHERJACKETS: Although slow-moving, these legless dark-grey grubs, the larvae of craneflies, feed at night on the roots of a variety of plants and can be troublesome in grass. Cover wet grass with black plastic or cardboard overnight. This should bring the larvae to the surface so that they can be removed.

MICE: Mice love peas and beans. Dampen seeds with paraffin before sowing if these creatures are going to be a problem.

MITES: Tiny mites such as the red spider variety will make strange patches on the underside of leaves, especially in a greenhouse, as they suck the sap from the plant, causing leaves to become yellow and mottled. The problem is worse in dry conditions, so spray plants with water regularly. In severe cases, use derris, one of the biodegradable 'botanical insecticides' that is widely available.

Snail

SLUGS AND SNAILS: Coming out at night from their hiding places under stones and debris, slugs and snails can eat their way through anything that gets in their slimy path. Amazingly, slugs come equipped with 15,000 tiny teeth. In between snacking on your hostas and destroying your hopes of home-grown lettuce, the female will lay a couple of thousand eggs, ensuring that the destruction will continue into the next generation. The chemical solution is the slug pellet but this can be lethal to birds and domestic pets. More natural methods of killing slugs include pouring salt on them so that they turn into a pool of water before your eyes, or sinking easily hidden yoghurt cartons filled with beer or milk into the soil. If they don't drink themselves to death, they will surely drown.

There is also some evidence that slugs don't like caffeine. Try spraying vulnerable plants with a very weak solution of coffee. Or place used coffee grains on the ground as a barrier. The only drawback is the effect the caffeine may have on beneficial insects. There is also a biological system that involves infecting the slugs with parasitic nematodes (parasites that infect and kill pests like slugs). These are sold in what looks like small blocks of soil. You mix this with water and spread it on the ground, but be warned – the soil must be warm if the parasites are to come alive. Another preventative method is to spread the area around a special plant with broken eggshells and small, sharp pebbles; slugs like to move on smooth ground. The cheapest method of all involves personal intervention. After watering your plants in the evening, come back about an hour later, when the slugs will have emerged. Pick them up and drop them into a bucket of salt water – or go on a crunching spree, not forgetting the baby white ones. This may be disgusting but it is effective, and birds will quickly devour what remains.

With climbing plants, such as clematis, wrap a sheet of cardboard or plastic around the base of the plant. Tie this loosely with string and smear grease on the top. Even if the slugs manage to climb up the cylinder, the grease will cause them to lose their grip and fall off again. Copper barriers can also be bought; these scare off slugs by giving them a mild shock.

My final advice? Avoid plants that slugs adore, such as hostas and lupins, and plant anything you really treasure well away from bushes, or climbers such as ivy.

 VINE WEEVILS: These white grubs like alpines, strawberries and pot plants and are among the most dreaded of garden pests. After the vine weevils have chomped their way through the plant's roots, it will quickly wilt and fall over. Turn over the soil and you will find great fat larvae with white bodies and brown heads. Destroy any you find and, for pot plants, make up a solution of derris and soak the entire pot in it. In warmer weather, the nematode *Heterorhabditis megidis* – a parasite – can be watered into suspect pots.

WASPS: These prey on greenfly, but will ravage the fruit crops and become extremely bad-tempered in autumn. Help them kill themselves by setting out a saucer of jam, or a glass of a soft drink in the garden. When they fall in, cover carefully and once they are definitely dead, dispose of them. To kill off a nest, pour petrol or paraffin into it and seal off the entrance.

WEEVILS: A common threat to apples and occasionally pears, weevils eat into the developing flower. If you look inside, you will find a grub or beetle in there. Remove it immediately.

WIREWORMS: Root crops, such as potatoes, can fall prey to these shiny beetle-like horrors that also attack the lower stems of chrysanthemums and tomatoes, leaving distinctive small holes. Regular digging will expose them, or you can put down pieces of potato or carrot to attract them. Then pick them off and destroy them.

WOODLICE: Woodlice hide in neglected corners and

come out at night to eat their way through seedlings and young plants. Keeping the garden tidy helps reduce their numbers.

The Gardener's Friends

Chemicals will get rid of troublesome insects. But they may also remove some of the good guys. The gardener's friends include:

BEES: Carry pollen from one plant to another.

BIRDS: Your worst enemy can also be your best friend. Birds such as robins, finches and tits will help you by eating large quantities of caterpillars and wireworms.

CENTIPEDES: Eat slugs and snails.

FROGS: Love to snack on slugs.

GROUND BEETLES: Also eat slugs and snails.

HOVERFLY: A small wasp-like insect, which, in its larval-stage, snacks on aphids. Flat, open flowers will attract them. Lace-wings and others wasps are also aphid eaters.

LADYBIRDS: Like nothing better than a sumptuous feast of aphids.

Other Problems

Insects are not the only problem you will have to deal with in the fight against nature. Leaves can develop mildew, blackspot, rust or streaks, while a white frothy spittle called cuckoo spit can appear on stems where a new shoot has grown. Potatoes are susceptible to scabs, wart disease or blight, and tomatoes to tomato-leaf mould. Apple trees get mildew and honey fungus.

On a more positive note, leaves can tell you a lot about the health of a plant and allow you to take preventative action. A red and yellow tint indicates a nitrogen shortage, yellow between the veins means that iron is needed, brown in the same place means a lack of magnesium, while scorched edges indicate a potash shortage. So here is another brief guide, this time to plant diseases. In all cases, remove the affected leaves, stems, or branches.

BLACK SPOT: A self-explanatory problem. Attacks roses, particularly those which have been heavily pruned.

BLIGHT: To save your potato crop, spray with Bordeaux mixture under and over the leaves every two weeks during hot, humid weather. Bordeaux mixture is made from copper sulphate and lime and is available from garden centres.

CANKER: On older trees and shrubs, the diseased branch can become cracked and swollen.

CLUBROOT: Roots end up as a messy slime after becoming swollen and distorted.

GREY MOULD: This is a fungus attacking leaves, stems and flowers, leaving them covered by a downy grey growth.

HONEY FUNGUS: A hugely destructive tree fungus that lives on dead tree stumps and roots. If you have it, you will see honey-coloured toadstools nearby.

MILDEW: Mildew, both the down and powder varieties, inhibits growth. It appears as a grey covering on the underside of leaves; remove these leaves immediately. Special sprays are available that do not affect fruit on trees.

RUST: This appears as bright orange, brown or black spots on leaves. It is the early stage of a fungal disease.

SILVER LEAF: This airborne fungus turns leaves silver and then brown and affects shoots and branches. These must all be removed to stop the disease spreading; if this doesn't work, the tree must be destroyed.

WEEDS: Even the best-kept garden will contain dandelions, couch grass, moss, plantain, bindweed, wild euphorbia and ragwort, all extremely hardy and fast-growing weeds. Their exuberance alone makes them easy enough to identify. Some are annuals, dying each season but leaving their seeds everywhere, while others are perennials with underground roots that seem impossible to remove entirely. The smallest piece of a dandelion root will regenerate; if only more prized specimens were as easy to grow. You don't really need to know the names of all the weeds in your garden; just make sure to keep them under control. This can be done the organic way by regular hoeing before the weeds mature; by pulling them up or digging them out once they become more established; or by pouring either salt or boiling water on them to see if that kills them. Wear gloves when pulling weeds and wash your hands carefully afterwards, as some can be highly noxious.

A mulch spread over cultivated beds will help smother annuals, which do not germinate if buried too deeply. Stones or pebbles are especially effective. Of course there are also weed-killers, coming in two broad varieties: those that target just the weeds and those that completely poison the soil, killing anything growing in it and possibly affecting animal and insect life. These should be used only as a last resort, if at all. After weeds have been removed, fork over the ground and dig in some manure or compost to replace lost nutrients.

Slug-Proof Plants

- ◆ Agapanthus
- ◆ Columbine
- ◆ Corydalis
- ◆ Foxgloves
- ◆ Grasses
- ◆ Poppies (Oriental and Icelandic)
- ◆ Verbascum

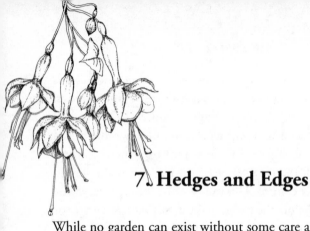

7. Hedges and Edges

While no garden can exist without some care and attention, a good hedge and a collection of well-spaced shrubs require little more than a trim one or twice a year and will always look good. The trick is to grow plants that you like, because some shrubs are so desperately dull that even a complete non-gardener will get bored looking at them.

The traditional green hedge is a valuable and relatively cheap addition to any property. Forming a natural and living boundary, it offers privacy, shelter and a backdrop for other plants and shrubs. But a hedge is not just a green wall; judiciously placed, hedges of varying height can divide and add interest, even to a small space.

In the traditional garden, the classic hedge consisted of beech, yew and tall conifers growing to 9m (30ft) and higher. Clearly, these are not always suitable for the ordinary urban garden, though you may find you have an old tree left untouched by the developers in some part of your garden, or even in the garden next door, which provides a ready-made screen.

A hedge should only be as tall as you need it. Before being tempted by one of the faster growers, remember that these will require the most hacking back later on. Unless the hedge is grown to provide shelter as well as screening, few people will want a hedge that grows more than about 165cms (5ft 6ins).

At this height, it will block the view of most motorists and pedestrians and is easy enough to clip.

What is the difference between a shrub and a tree? A tree has only one stem at ground level with everything else springing from that. A shrub has several woody stems at ground level. Planting a continuous line of shrubs or trees creates a hedge, a word that comes from the old English *hegge*, meaning enclosure. Most people opt for an evergreen hedge that retains its leaves over the winter. There is plenty of choice. Virtually all the conifers are evergreen, while other popular hedging shrubs, such as privet, are semi-evergreen, keeping many of their leaves in a mild winter. Think of going for a mixture of plants rather than just one variety, especially if you live in a housing estate where heavy hedging looks inappropriate and oppressive.

With or without traditional hedging, every garden should start with a variety of contrasting evergreens to give it interest throughout the year. Colours can range from the dark green and red of photinia 'Red Robin', to the silver grey senecio and the variegated oleaster. Then there is the vast collection of hebes; these come in plain green, as well as in various shades of pink and purple. Heather is another popular shrub with many gardeners. Growing habits differ greatly – some shrubs grow up, while others spread. Just because it is an evergreen does not mean it has to be just one dull colour of green.

If you have moved into an old house, you will probably inherit a number of well-established shrubs and a particular style of hedging. In my case, it was a fifty-year old griselinia. I know this particular plant grows fast, forms an effective screen and is inexpensive, but I loathe its shiny green blandness. On one side, the hedge was over 3m (10ft) high and ran about an arm's length, with the remaining space filled with a large and overgrown heather and two dwarf conifers, one light green and the other dark and dying. No space was left to plant anything new and, after a few years, I decided they all had to go. The heather pulled up easily and the soft-wood conifers I chopped down myself, but removing the griselinia proved a serious challenge. The main root had turned into a thick trunk about a metre in girth and after everything green was removed by chainsaw, needed the attention of a small digger at considerable cost. Other smaller roots had spread quite a distance under the lawn. It left me thinking hard about the need for any hedging at all in suburbia.

Traditionally, late autumn was the time for establishing new hedges. It made sense, giving the new plants a chance to settle in, enjoy the autumn and winter rain, and develop roots before the summer. Nowadays, hedges can be 'bought in' at any time of the year, but sticking to the traditional time-scale will pay off and can be a lot cheaper if you can find a market gardener prepared to sell you the plants in their bare-rooted state. You can also cut costs by putting down just a few plants at first and then, when autumn comes around again, taking hard-wood cuttings.

For a temporary screen over the summer, plant the quick-growing summer cypress or 'Burning Bush' (*Kochia*), a neat bush with feathery leaves that turn purple, bronze or red in autumn, when you can put in something more permanent.

It is important to plan your hedge. Think hard before you decide on a style, because once planted, it will not be easy to remove, as my experience proves. Decide what you want, buy the plants or take sufficient cuttings from others already in the garden, and make sure you have enough to fill the space. Mark out the stretch you need to dig, using flour, lime or a piece of garden string tied to sticks. Dig out a trench about 60cms (2ft) wide and after forking in plenty of manure or compost, add some powdered organic fertilizer.

Now, stretch a piece of garden string through the centre of the trench to help position your plants. If you want a particularly thick hedge, plant a double row. Use a ruler, or a piece of cut cane, to help keep the space between the plants even as you put them in. Re-fill the trench, firming in the plants, and water well. For the first season, you will have to pay close attention to your growing hedge, watering it as carefully as you would any other plants in your garden. A young tree or shrub has yet to develop strong roots that can tap deep and wide into the soil for moisture and, if it gets too weak from thirst, will become a magnet for an assortment of nasties, such as sap-sucking aphids. A mulch spread around the base of the young plants in the summer will help retain moisture. You will also have to do the usual weeding, although as the hedge develops, this problem will vanish – one of the main reasons people like hedges.

If you already have a garden wall or fence, a full hedge may not be necessary. Stand alone plants, such as a holly tree or a rhododendron, or climbers, ranging from ivy and virginia creeper to honeysuckle and clematis, will help you make the best of a dull wall and form a green backdrop for your borders. Be careful with colours: a yellow plant such as some of the varieties of privet or cypress, can be limiting and will clash with a red-brick house, while purple and too much dark green can be gloomy. Mix and match.

For a trouble-free garden, look no further than a range of standard shrubs. There is nothing to growing these, especially if you plant in autumn – prepare the soil, dig a hole, throw in some compost, stick in the plant, water well, and there you are. For the summer after, keep watering and weeding. Most of the popular shrubs then take on a life of their own and can be ignored, though some are invasive and need regular cutting back. However, if you are a person of taste and discrimination, you may find it annoying that every other garden around, including office parks and garage forecourts, has an identical display – a few cotoneasters, a rampant olearia, a conifer, a few clumps of grasses and heathers and, if they are adventurous, a fuchsia or two, all surrounded by a pebble mulch. So look around before you buy and do try out a few different plants. If you find you do not like them as they grow, just dig them up and throw them on the compost heap.

Top Choices for Hedges

This is not a comprehensive list. The plants are mostly ones I have dealt with myself or would like to. The common name is used first, followed by the Latin if this is different, as few plants in garden centres seem to be called by what we know them. Any shrub that grows to over 1.80m (6ft) can be used in an informal hedge; there is no rule that says all hedges must be made of box, yew or privet. Conifers are the other popular choice, either one or two, judiciously placed, or an entire run of them. Whatever you do, use your imagination!

BEECH (*Fagus*): Although the common beech, or *F. sylvatica*, a deciduous tree, will grow to over 30m (100ft), it is still a popular choice for hedging because hard pruning does it no harm. The stunning foliage, which stays on the tree even in winter, turns gold, bronze and then a distinctive withered brown.

BOX (*Buxus, buxaceae*): Box, with its small, glossy leaves, and tiny light-green flowers, is one of the more popular hedging plants and these days is often sold in a tub, tightly clipped into ball or pyramid shapes, like a plant form of poodle. An evergreen, it comes in around 30 varieties of shrub and small tree and is particularly good as a low, neat hedge. Extremely hardy, box is long-lived and can reach a height of 9m (30ft). It tolerates heavy pruning, which is why it is so popular with topiary enthusiasts. Put down in autumn or spring, spacing the plants 45cms (18ins) apart, or just 15cms (6ins) apart if using the dwarf variety. Box can be propagated from cuttings in late summer or autumn. After five years, it will reach a height of 60-90cms (2-3ft).

ESCALLONIA: With its shiny leaves and tiny pink and white blooms, the evergreen escallonia is a useful shrub that grows quickly into a substantial screen and is especially good in coastal areas. The hardy 'Donard' hybrids are particularly popular and can be seen in many gardens. Escallonia takes to most soils and does not mind some shade, making it a good, all-purpose plant. Trim after flowering as it can grow upwards and outwards to about 3m (10ft).

FORSYTHIA: The bright yellow of the forsythia, or golden bells plant, signals the end of winter and adds an irresistible blaze of colour to the spring garden. But although attractive at that time of year, the flowerless forsythia can look bony and bedraggled. I would use it judiciously and maybe plant a clematis through it to disguise its bareness over the summer. Just sow the clematis in the ground below; it will use the forsythia as a natural support. There are a number of varieties of forsythia and some, such as 'Lynwood', are prized for their abundant flowers. For those with less space, 'Bronxensis' will reach just 60cms (2ft) in height, and flowers when other varieties are past their best. Plant your forsythia in a sunny or partially shaded site and propagate by means of cuttings from new growth. It will grow fast in any reasonable soil, typically reaching a height of about 2.4m (8ft) after five years. Cut back only long shoots that have flowered; too severe a hacking will mean a poor show of flowers the following year.

HAWTHORN (*Crataegus*): More strictly defined as a tree, the native hawthorn can make an excellent hedge and grows in any kind of soil with the minimum of fuss. It can withstand almost anything, from city pollution to driving winds, and provides a welcoming haven for bird and insect life. Hawthorns will produce flowers in spring and berries or 'haws' in autumn. The common hawthorn (*C. monogyna*) is widely used for hedges and is easily grown, while 'Paul's Scarlet' also grows quickly to form a thick, thorny screen. To grow a hedge, plant young trees 60cms (18-24ins) apart. Trim away weak growth to show off flowers, foliage and berries, remembering to wear a thick pair of gloves.

HOLLY (*Ilex*): If you are thinking of security, then holly with its prickly leaves, is a natural deterrent. It is also an attractive winter plant with bright red berries that a female plant will continue to produce as long as you plant a male specimen nearby. The berries act as a magnet for birds, while the plant is also home to the holly blue butterfly. After a slow start, holly grows moderately quickly and can be cut back hard without damage. It prefers a good, fertile soil and, as might be expected from a plant associated with the Northern hemisphere and Christmas, dislikes too much sun and heat. Apart from the traditional *Ilex aquifolium*, there are a number of other hollies worth seeking out – 'Golden King' (*I. x altaclerensis*), a female variety despite the name, has broader yellow-speckled leaves and is not as prickly as traditional varieties. It grows slowly at a rate of about 1.2m (4ft) every five years but can eventually reach a height of 6m (20ft). 'Silver Queen' (*I. aquifolium* 'Silver Queen'), a male, is worth planting nearby to ensure an annual show of berries.

HORNBEAM (*Carpinus betalus*): Although not as popular as the beech, the hornbeam grows faster and is tougher. It thrives in any soil, can withstand some pollution and has an attractive grey, fluted trunk, good colouring in autumn, and hanging clusters of hop-like fruits. *C. betalus* 'Fastigiata' is smaller.

JAPANESE ROSE (*Rosa rugosa*): This densely growing rose has prickly stems, wrinkled foliage that turns gold in autumn, and large pink flowers blooming right through the summer. It also produces attractive round, red hips and is particularly suited to seaside gardens. It will reach a height of about 2m (6ft) after eight years.

LEYLAND CYPRESS (*x Cupressocyparis leylandii*): The fastest-growing conifer of them all, the leyland cypress is the first choice for a fast-growing hedge. But do you really want a plant that will grow to a dense 10m (30ft) in less than ten years? It would, of course, be perfect if you live on a noisy street and have a long front garden. Far more popular for the more compact garden are the many varieties of false cypress (*Chamaecyparis*). These come in all sizes, from rockery dwarfs to 1.80m (6ft) trees, and their foliage can vary from grey to yellow. They prefer a moist, well-drained soil in a sheltered site and should be trimmed back regularly to keep them dense.

OLEASTER (*Elaeagnus*): Coming in both evergreen and deciduous varieties, the oleaster, with fragrant flowers appearing from June, can grow up to 5m (15ft) and will survive even the worst of winters. With its colourful yellow-splashed leaves, the *E. pungens Maculta* can provide good contrast in the evergreen border and needs little attention.

PHOTINIA RED ROBIN (*Photinia x fraserei* 'Red Robin'): This variety of photinia will turn into an eye-catching addition to your garden and is a personal favourite, mainly because of a gorgeous and beautifully trimmed specimen in a garden near me. Originally from China, the 'Red Robin' variety of photinia first appeared in New Zealand. The narrow, shiny leaves are bright red in spring, before turning bronze and then deep green, but year round, there will be rich green leaves on the lower half of the bush and deep red on top. A bonus on untrimmed bushes is the show of white flowers. It tolerates alkaline soils and is considered hardy, though susceptible to frost in spring. One shrub can make a substantial hedge, growing to about 6m (20ft) and spreading about 4m (12ft), though it does take a while to establish itself and needs judicious trimming. Other recommended photinias are the hardy *P.* 'Robusta' and *P. beauverdiana*, which produces dark red berries.

PRIVET (*Ligustrum*): Not the best regarded plant in the garden centre these days, but privet, which comes in more than one variety, does have its uses. It flourishes in any kind of soil, does not object to some shade, and apart from a trim in May and August, needs little attention. It is, however, susceptible to honey fungus and, once established, its aggressive root system goes everywhere, sucking the goodness from nearby soil. A good tip is to drive a spade down into the roots all along the length to slow down growth.

YEW (*Taxus baccata*): The classic evergreen yew hedge is seen in all the best classical gardens. It is extremely hardy, grows about 30cms (1ft) a year, needs only one clipping each season and is happy in shade. Even when cut right to the ground, it will grow back again, and it is ideal for topiary. Yew comes in a number of varieties, with green, yellow or variegated foliage, all extremely poisonous.

Climbers

CLEMATIS: Clematis, a vigorous climber that comes in over 300 varieties, is a bestseller in any garden centre. Beautiful and adaptable, clematis comes in an assortment of colours, from white and yellow to pink and mauve, and you can find one that will bloom at almost any time of the year. All clematis like the sun, but prefer their roots in the shade. They will grow well on a shaded wall so long as their flowers are in sunlight. They like moist, slightly alkaline soil and need plenty of feeding, plus mulching in warm weather to help keep the roots cool. Plant them at least 30cms (1ft) from stone, brick or concrete walls that can reflect heat, and dig in plenty of compost before planting. If your plant is only blooming on top, pinch out the growing tips of new stems in spring to encourage flowers to develop lower down.

As it grows, your clematis will need support and will cling to anything, from netting to bushes. Tie new stems to a trellis or use a system of vine eyes and wires. An annual pruning will also be necessary. There are three main groups of clematis: the first consists of the evergreens and early flowering species that need pruning after early flowering. The second group covers the early and mid-season single-flowered hybrids and the double and semi-double hybrids, pruned back hard in the spring, while the third consists of clematis varieties that flower late, needing hard pruning in winter.

The choice truly is bewildering. An especially striking species is the clematis *alpina*, with its silky seed heads and purple-blue flowers in spring, while for those who like yellow blooms, the clematis *tangutica* flowers from midsummer until autumn and can be trained over a wall. There are also a few hardy herbaceous species that are excellent for the border.

HONEYSUCKLE (*Lonicera*): Honeysuckle, with its masses of colourful droopy blooms and heavenly scent, can grow quickly and, if not cut back, is strong enough to pull a trellis off the wall. A climber that needs support, honeysuckle is quite happy in partial shade and, unlike clematis, does not need sun on its stems. But no one could describe it as a tidy plant and it will look best when trained over an arch or pergola. Most varieties have fragrant blooms and can be propagated by taking cuttings in the summer. The native honeysuckle or woodbine (*L. periclymenum*) produces its red and cream flowers from June to August. Another variety, *L. japonica*, with yellow blooms, flowers longer and keeps its leaves over the winter. Not all varieties come scented, so check when you buy. Honeysuckles will grow about 3m (10ft) in five years.

IVY (*Hedera*): No one can deny the versatility of the common ivy, although the darker varieties can get a bit overwhelming and gloomy if not controlled. An evergreen, which makes it unusual among climbers, ivy comes in a huge selection of varieties and colours, grows anywhere, and will cover an ugly wall in a matter of years. It is also an effective ground-cover plant. On a wall, the common ivy (*H. helix*) in any of its cultivars, such as 'Buttercup', 'Goldheart', 'Hibernica' or 'Marmorata', will grow 30m (100ft) and spread 6m (20ft). Although by itself it will not damage a wall, ivy needs hard pruning so that its sheer weight does not become a problem.

POLYGONUM: Sold in garden centres as 'Mile-a-Minute' plant, the *polygonum*, known also as Russian vine (*P. baldschuanicum*) or knotweed (*P. aubertii*), grows about 5m (15ft) a year and produces masses of small, white flowers from July onward. It can grow to 12m (40ft) and spread 30m (100ft), so will soon smother any garden eyesore, but that is its only virtue. Once rampant, this plant is extremely difficult to control and neighbours will not thank you if it spreads into their garden. A classic case of easy-to-grow not being the best option.

VIRGINIA CREEPER (*Parthenocissus*): Not the cheapest of choices, a classic virginia creeper can be unpredictable in its growth patterns and could take a while to establish. So even if it looks dead, leave it alone for a few seasons. It will need support at first but will soon start using its tendrils to stick to the wall. A deciduous plant, the leaves turns a fiery red in autumn before falling off. It likes fertile soil and a bit of warmth, but can produce a good display on a cool, shady wall. The commonly entitled 'Boston Ivy' (*P. tricuspidata*) is the one you see everywhere and has smaller leaves than the traditional 'True Virginia Creeper' (*P. quinquefolia*). This will reach a height of 20m (40ft) if left, alone so it may need some pruning in spring. To make an instant hedge, let a creeper grow over a simple screen of posts and wire netting. Before planting at a wall, prepare a large bed of at least 60cms (2ft) as the soil near walls can be poor. To encourage the plant to 'stick', tie shoots to a piece of trellis or netting until the plant starts to cling to the wall on its own. Keep the new plant well watered and feed the entire bed and the roots underneath in spring.

WISTERIA: With its hanging tassels of flowers and its twisting trunk and stems, wisteria is a plant that simply takes your breath away, though you may prefer to admire its elegance and majesty from afar. The wisteria is not a plant that tolerates competition, overpowering anything grown nearby, and as it will flourish for up to one hundred years, it is going to be around for a while. If you decide to take responsibility for one of these spectacular beauties, choose your variety carefully. The popular *W. sinensis* is a rampant grower with long flowers that could get into your gutters and is capable of lifting the roof off your house. A far better choice is one of the varieties from the less vigorous *W. floribunda* or Japanese wisteria family, such as the 'Multijuga' (*W. floribunda* 'Multijuga'), with long 60cms (2ft) flowers in two shades of lilac appearing in early spring. There is also a more unusual white-flowering variety called 'Alba' (*W. floribunda* 'Alba'). These can be grown close to a wall or over a pergola.

Wisteria need a sunny position and they should be trained horizontally with a vine eye and wire system. Plant about 30cms (1ft) from a wall in spring or autumn, after digging in plenty of good compost. Cut the leading shoot back to the height of the first wire and, as side shoots develop, train them along the wire, remembering to take one shoot upwards. Prune after early flowering in July, cutting back shoots by one-third of their growth, and again in early winter, leaving just two buds on each new shoot. After five years, your wisteria should have grown to 6m (20ft).

Shrubs

BAMBOO: Despite its exotic origins, bamboo is classified as a shrub and will grow in partial shade and ordinary soil. Indeed, some varieties can take over the garden if you are not careful and should be avoided unless you are aiming to grow your own jungle.

If you admire the distinctive hollow canes (officially called culms) and graceful, evergreen foliage, there are more restrained varieties of bamboo. The *Fargesia murieliae* or umbrella bamboo, for instance, like all in the *fargesia* family, grows in a neat clump and will not stray. It will, however, need a carefully chosen spot in the garden, as it will spread about 1.5m (5ft) and can reach a height of 4m (13ft). Another clump-forming variety worth seeking out is the black bamboo (*Phyllostachys nigra*). For casual gardeners, the good news is that bamboos need very little attention and, in the right location, can be used as a screen, with the great advantage that they need no clipping (although the centre of the plant should be cleared of old canes in spring). Bamboos will also thrive in containers, though they will need dividing after a few years. The bad news is that the best examples can be very expensive.

BERBERIS: The prickly shrub berberis, or barberry, comes in many varieties, some of them small enough for a rock garden, or ground cover, others growing to 3m (10ft) and suitable for hedging. There are dozens of both evergreen and deciduous varieties, all with spiny leaves and producing small flowers and berries. In an evergreen like *B. darwinii*, a good choice for hedging, the shiny foliage resembles holly leaves, and deep yellow flowers in spring are followed by purple berries. Of the deciduous types, *B. thunbergii* grows to less than 1.8m (6ft) and has bright red autumn leaves and berries. The colour of the leaves varies according to the variety. Tough and hardy, a carefully selected berberis can provide interest all year round. It will grow in almost any soil, providing it is not too alkaline, and it likes plenty of sun.

BROOM (*Cytisus*): A plant that prefers poor soil, broom is grown for the tiny delicate flowers that completely cover its arching stems. These can be yellow, white or red. All brooms need pruning every year.

BUDDLEIA (*Buddleja*): The fast-growing buddleia or butterfly bush, is another shrub you will find in the gardens all around you, usually in the long-tailed purple variety, which flowers from early August. This is greatly attractive to butterflies, thanks to its honey scent, and will grow in well-drained soil with plenty of sun.

Although dull, buddleia can serve as space filler and as a backdrop to other plants in a sunny border, where they can grow to about 2.8m (9ft). For those with an aversion to purple flowers and lots of pruning, the variety called the 'Orange Ball Tree' (*B. globosa*) produces masses of small, round orange flowers. Standard buddleias must be pruned back hard in March, or they will take over your border. They will also scatter their seed everywhere, so beware.

CALIFORNIAN LILAC (*Ceanothus*): The fast-growing Californian lilac, with its distinctive blue flowers and year-round dark foliage, has become widely available in recent years and can be gorgeous in the right spot, although it has a short life of just twenty years. Coming in deciduous and evergreen varieties, it needs sun and well-drained soil and the evergreen varieties are not fully hardy. As with most frost-haters, the plant needs a sunny, sheltered spot where it will get some protection from winter weather. With a few canes or trellis for support, the climbing varieties will reach up to 1.8m (6ft) in five years. After the flowers bloom in May, cut out the shoots that have flowered. This will keep the bush compact and prolong its life. Choose a spot for your ceanothus carefully – this is a plant that does not like to be moved once it is settled. In winter, cover with an old blanket or horticultural fleece if frost is forecast, remembering to take it off in the morning. 'Blue Mound' for ground cover, along with 'Autumnal Blue' and 'Puget Blue', are three of the best varieties.

COTINUS: Known as the smoke bush or tree, cotinus is grown for its spectacular autumn colours, its foliage turning brilliant red, yellow, orange and purple, especially when planted in less rich soils. The only problem is matching its intense colours with other plants, as it will grow to 4m (13ft) in time.

COTONEASTER: The cotoneaster, originally from China, is supposed to be one of the toughest plants you could buy, but my own first specimen died. Moving it around once too often probably did not help. The variety I bought is the tall one with weeping stems fanning out from the main trunk (*C. hybridus pendulus*). Like all cotoneasters, it has small, green leaves and red berries and produces small, white flowers in spring. I also have a ground cover variety (*C. horizontalis*), which, oddly, does nothing to discourage weeds, forcing me to root underneath it to get at them. But since it is now growing strongly up the back wall, I may put up with it.

FUCHSIA: The bell-like flowers of the fuchsia, flowering from July until October and later, make it second only to the rose in the affections of gardeners. Originally from South America, fuchsia comes in many varieties, some growing upwards, some providing ground cover and others more suitable to hanging baskets. A deciduous plant, fuchsia needs a fertile soil and is one of the easiest of plants to propagate by cuttings during the summer. The hardiest species are in the *F. magellanica* family, some growing up to 2m (6ft) in frost-free areas, and suitable for use as a hedge. Most have the distinctive scarlet bells with purple or cream petals. The hybrid fuchsias have some splendid names: 'Mrs Popple', 'Madame Cornellissen' and 'Chillerton Beauty' among them. These will grow in a sunny spot with some shade and reach heights of 1.5m (5ft) and a spread of 1.2m (4ft). Prune back hard in spring.

HEATHER (*Calluna* or *Erica*): Heathers come in two broad varieties, though purists insist that only *Calluna vulgaris* or 'ling' and its derivatives are true heathers. All others are 'heaths'. *Calluna*, the common heather of northern and western European moors, is a lime-hater and loves the sun. If you have acid soil and a sunny aspect, there is an enormous variety in all heights and shapes and in colours ranging from white (*C. vulgaris* 'Kinlochruel') to brilliant red (*C. vulgaris* 'Sunset') to chose from. 'H.E. Beale', with long spikes of pink flowers, is one of the most popular varieties.

The *Erica* species of heather is even larger and includes over 700 varieties. While a handful of peat mixed in with the soil is recommended at planting time, some varieties, such as *E. x darleyensis*, *E. carnea* and *E. erigena*, will grow anywhere. Plant all heathers deeply and water well. Both species of heather benefit from a trim in spring.

HEBE: A sun-loving evergreen, hebe, or shrubby veronica, comes in many varieties, although the most common are neat, compact bushes with glossy leaves and small blue or white flowers on spikes. The hybrid 'Autumn Glory' and the variety *H. brachysiphon* are popular for good reason, as they are hardy and reliable and thrive in most locations, although they will need to be protected from frost. In general, the smaller the leaf, the hardier the variety. With hebes, there is plenty of choice: from the plain green non-flowering *H. cupressoides* 'Boughton Dome', to the popular 'Great Orme' with its pink flowers, the violet-blue of 'Quicksilver' and the lilac flowers and crimson-tinged foliage of *H. x franciscana* 'Blue Gem'. In cooler locations, plant your hebes close to a wall or fence, preferably facing south or west. Hebes should be planted in spring so that they will be well established before the following winter. They have a shallow root system and will need plenty of watering in the first year. Take cuttings in July so that if the plant dies over the winter, you can start again.

HYDRANGEA: With their big lace-cap or mop-head flowers, hydrangeas grow well in partial shade, making them useful for a north-facing garden. All that is needed then is to remove the flower heads after the winter. Even if you find the standard varieties a bit blowsy, have a look at *H. aspera*, with its soft, bristly leaves and looser flower heads, pale blue on the outside and pink mauve inside. This hardy plant can climb to 2.5m (8ft) and flowers from June to August.

JAPONICA (*Chaenomeles*): An old favourite, japonica, or flowering quince, is grown for its spring flowers and its autumn fruits. A deciduous plant that loves the sun, it can tolerate light shade, flourishes in ordinary soil, and is suitable for training against a wall. In spring, it produces rose-like flowers in different colours, depending on the variety, followed by yellow-green fruits in autumn. A stunning example is 'Crimson and Gold' with its extrovert pillar-box red flowers.

JASMINE (*Jasminum*): With its tubular yellow flowers, winter jasmine (*J. nudiflorum*) provides welcome off-season colour to the garden. Although not a true climber, its long stems will grow up to 1m (40ins) in length and can be draped over an unsightly barrel or bank or trained up a trellis. Jasmine will grow in any soil and will flourish even against a north-facing wall. In March, prune back the shoots that flowered. For summer flowering, the common white jasmine (*J. officinale*), a climber that can reach 9m (30ft) tall, keeps going until the autumn.

KERRIA: For some reason also known as 'Jew's Mallow', kerria is a popular trouble-free shrub, with light green leaves, usually producing yellow flowers in the spring. It will grow to about 1.80m (6ft) in any soil but needs some protection from wind. Prune back flowering shoots in June. The 'Plenifora' variety will produce double blooms in bright yellow.

LILAC (*Syringa*): The fancy-flowered and heavy-scented lilac is a mainstay of the mixed border, despite having a short flowering season of just three weeks from May onwards. Varieties of the 'Common Lilac' (*S. vulgaris*) will grow in most conditions but need feeding and mulching annually as well as judicious pruning to remove old growth and dead flowers. Chalky soils are best, though lilacs can flourish anywhere. If you find the ordinary lilac a bit flashy, try *S. microphylla* with its small leaves and delicate clusters of pink flowers.

MAGNOLIA: The magnolia is an elegant beauty – gorgeous goblet-like white, pink or red flowers, a rich scent, an eye-catching stem system, and foliage that turns a distinctive brown in autumn. Magnolias are thought to be difficult, but apart from a dislike of chalky soil and a need for some shade, are not that fussy, if given a rich, well-prepared bed and a sunny position. If you see them growing in your neighbourhood, then by all means give them a try. It is important not to disturb a magnolia's roots once planted and, as these stay close to the surface, to dig with care around them. The most impressive magnolia is really a tree, *M. grandiflora*, that will eventually reach a height of 15m (50ft). It produces large, creamy white blooms from July. Not quite as large but still capable of reaching 9m (30ft) is *M. x soulangeana*, a spreading bush producing its distinctive creamy pink flowers in April, before the leaves appear. Suitable for small gardens and tubs is *M. stellata*, producing bursts of star-like white flowers in early spring and growing no more than 3.5m (12ft).

MAHONIA: With attractive dark green foliage, dense clusters of fragrant yellow flowers early in the year, and small grape-like berries later on, mahonias provide year-round interest in the garden. Most popular variety is probably *M. x media* 'Charity', an upright shrub that will end up an eye-catching 3m (10ft) tall. *M. japonica* is another easy-to-find variety that has darker foliage and more pendulous clusters of flowers. *M. aquifolium* 'Oregon Grape' is used as ground cover under trees, while *M. x wagneri Undulata*, if you can find it, makes a good specimen tree in a sunny spot. Mahonias grow anywhere and little pruning is necessary.

MEXICAN ORANGE FLOWER (*Choisya*): A firm favourite, this neat, fragrant evergreen shrub with glossy green leaves and star-shaped white flowers will flourish in all conditions. Coming in just one variety, it flowers first in April and then intermittently until December. It will reach a height of up to 3m (10ft) and needs no pruning. Its one drawback is that it can be sensitive to frost, so in colder districts, plant it against a wall.

OLEASTER (*Elaeagnus*): A plant that is grown for its attractive, glossy foliage, there are deciduous and evergreen versions of oleaster, with semi-evergreen varieties such as *E. x ebbingei* 'Gilt Edge' reaching a height of up to 3m (10ft) and having distinctive yellow-edged leaves. The evergreen species *E. pungens* is more spreading, with 'Maculata' one of the best-known varieties, its dark green leaves coming with a distinctive gold streak in the centre. Will grow anywhere.

PHYGELIUS: With its exotic pillar-box red flowers, shaped like drooping hunting horns, the 'African Queen' variety of phygelius (*P. x rectus* 'African Queen'), or Cape fuchsia, deserves more recognition, especially as it is completely hardy and can be pruned back easily in spring. Originally from South Africa, phygelius will quickly form a thicket and, as it grows to about 90cm (3ft) it its first year, can be mixed successfully with other shrubs to form an attractive low-lying hedge in a sunny, well-drained site. Other varieties of phygelius include 'Yellow Trumpet' (*P. aequalis* 'Yellow Trumpet') with yellow flowers.

POTENTILLA: Potentilla, or shrubby cinquefoil, flowers from May until December, reason enough to plant it in any border, where it makes an ideal partner for lavender or roses.

The small flowers, in a variety of colours, are plentiful though not particularly eye-catching. It will grow in any well-drained soil, in sun or in partial shade, and reaches about knee height. Among the varieties are 'Abbotswood' with gleaming, white flowers, 'Gibson's Scarlet' with a profusion of red flowers, and 'Elizabeth', with canary yellow blossoms. Potentilla is available as a shrub or a perennial and benefits from light pruning in spring.

PYRACANTHA: Since the development of new disease-resisting strains, the pyracantha, or firethorn, has once again become a favourite. It resembles the cotoneaster, but the leaves are toothed, the stems extra spiny and there are both red- and yellow-berried versions. Left in an open spot, it will grow into a large 3m (10ft) bush but it is now most often grown as a wall shrub that will spread quite a distance. Pyracantha will flourish in any soil, can tolerate some shade and needs cutting back after flowering. Birds love the berries, but the needle-like spines make this plant a bit of a hazard and it should be carefully placed.

RHODODENDRON, AZALEA: There are simply thousands of different species and hybrids loosely gathered under the name rhododendron. One species, that of azalea, is now considered a distinct group, because it is mostly deciduous and has more delicate stems and blooms. So if you think you do not like this particular plant, which in some habitats is considered a weed, you may have been looking at the wrong one. Different varieties will produce almost every colour imaginable, and the flowers are not all necessarily those large feather dusters. What they all have in common is evergreen and lance-shaped foliage. To grow any type of rhododendron, including azaleas, an acid soil is vital. So if your soil is average and you want to grow them, dig in plenty of peat before planting; otherwise, the foliage will turn yellow. Hard pruning is needed in April as well as the usual deadheading.

RIBES: Easy to grow in any reasonable soil, the ornamental currant or ribes produces pale pink flowers in March and is a popular choice for early season gardens. To stand out from the crowd, pick a more unusual variety, such as 'Pulborough Scarlet' or 'King Edward VII', both of them producing bright, scarlet blossoms.

ROCK ROSE (*Cistus*): The rock, or sun, rose, native to the Mediterranean, comes as a hardy evergreen with pretty flowers that bloom in spring. Among the recommended varieties are 'Grayswood Pink', a dense, hardy shrub with small pale pink flowers and grey green foliage. 'Elma' has larger white flowers and deep green leaves, while *C. crispus*, another hardy variety, has deep red flowers.

ST JOHN'S WORT (*Hypericum*): This low-growing semi-evergreen bush has lost out to senecio in the easy-growing fashion stakes, but with its darker foliage and cheerful yellow flowers, it is just as attractive. Like senecio, it will grow almost anywhere, including under trees, but it is not quite as invasive and you will get several shows of flowers over a summer. The 'Hidcote' is the usual variety, but there are several others worth investigating, such as 'Elstead', with egg-shaped fruits after flowering, and the tall 'Rowallane' that bears an abundance of large yellow flowers from July. Prune most varieties back almost to ground level in spring.

SENECIO: The common senecio perennial, with its attractive grey foliage and daisy-like flowers, can play a vital role in brightening the winter garden, but it needs attention, as it grows rapidly, smothering anything that gets in its way. Hack it back every April and you will have a neat, manageable plant that complements hebes and dark-leaved laurels. Although senecio does not mind wind and spray, it is not completely hardy and prefers a sheltered sunny spot.

SNOWBERRY (*Symphoricarpos*): The common snowberry, with its large, marble-like berries, is a common choice for covering a neglected area in the garden and thrives in sun or shade. It produces white flowers in spring, followed by its distinctive berries in autumn. But beware – this deciduous shrub is rampant once it gets started and unwanted shoots must be removed in spring. Try non-suckering hybrids such as *S. x doorenbosii* 'Magic Berry' for rich pink or 'Mother of Pearl' for white berries.

SPIRAEA: Easy-to-cultivate and growing masses of flowers, spiraea is a group of quick-growing twiggy shrubs, related to the rose. The spring-flowering types, such as 'Bridal Wreath' (*S. arguta*), produce small white blossoms on attractive, arching stems, while the summer varieties, such as 'Anthony Waterer' , are usually pink or red, the flowers appearing as either round domes or upright spikes. Hard pruning, right back to ground level, is essential with the summer varieties if the plant is not to turn into a thicket. Spiraea grows in any reasonably rich soil and tolerates partial shade.

SUMACH (*Rhus*): A deciduous plant grown for its brilliant autumn hues, long spikes of small crimson fruits, and architectural stem system. The 'Stag's Horn' (*R. typhina*), which almost qualifies as a small tree, will grow anywhere sunny to a height of 3.6m (12ft), but its prolific suckering habit, while great for propagation purposes, makes it unsuitable for a lawn. Stems should be cut back to 30cms (1ft) in spring.

VIBERNUM: A large and versatile family of deciduous and evergreen shrubs, with varieties that will suit almost any purpose and provide year-round colour, vibernum are all hardy and easy to grow. The winter-flowering group includes the ubiquitous *V. tinus*, with its laurel-like leaves, which produces clusters of pink buds, followed by white flowers from

December. The spring-flowering group, including *V. opulus sterile*, have 'snowball' shaped blossoms, while *V. carlessii* has more delicate, tubular blooms that are very fragrant. Then there is the autumn group, with *V. davidii* flowering from June and producing blue berries later in the year, and *V. opulus* with its fiery red foliage and red berries. Viburnum does best in full sun and prefers well-cultivated or even chalky soils. Old or damaged branches should be cut back in spring, but otherwise it does not need pruning.

WEIGELA: Sometimes listed as diervilla, weigela produces arching stems of undistinguished pink tubular flowers in May. It does best when pruned annually and grown in rich soil, but it will grow almost anywhere. If you plant one, go for something a bit more unusual, such as the 'Bristol Ruby' variety, with its ruby red blooms.

Five Favourite Shrubs

- *Mahonia* 'Charity'
- *Phygelius* 'African Queen'
- *Photinia* 'Red Robin'
- *Hebe* 'Blue Gem'
- *Ceanothus* 'Blue Mound'

---

8. Tree Thoughts

If they could talk, most trees could tell a story. Apart from their obvious location in forests, remarkable trees are found in parks, farms, estates, graveyards and backyards all over the country. The oldest living plant on the planet is a 12,000-year-old redwood. Some trees are huge, like American redwoods and oaks, others are simply beautiful, such as the best examples of cedars and willows.

Trees are the lungs of the planet, soaking up excess carbon dioxide and other greenhouse gases from the atmosphere and neutralising them. In countries such as Bangladesh, Nepal and Brazil, trees help keep the shifting earth in place. Unfortunately, their vital role was only realised after profit-driven developers cut down the tropical rain forests, resulting in disastrous flooding and freak landslides. In cities, as well as filtering and purifying the air we breathe, trees help cut down on noise pollution and hide some of the more brutal examples of modern architecture. Even more vitally, they play their part in the great cycle of being by providing food, nesting sites and shelter for wildlife. Native trees are particularly important to any country, since over the millennia, they have adapted to their local environment. For example, in Britain and Ireland, a native oak supports 280 species of plant, animal and insect life and a willow is not too far behind, hosting 266 species. An imported pine supports just seven species of life, while the horse chestnut, another non-native, is only favoured by four species.

Unfortunately every year, thousands of city trees die through neglect, disease and over-development. Every street needs trees, although all too often young saplings fall victim to vandalism or traffic. If you can, get your local council to plant a few trees on your road, in any nearby piece of waste ground, or in your local school. If they aren't co-operative, get a few neighbours involved and do it yourselves. It will soften the harsh look of the concrete jungle and you will have a thing of beauty to observe and nurture as it grows. Not only that, but long after you are gone, future generations will thank you.

For advice on planting a native tree, contact an organisation such as Conservation Volunteers. Every autumn, it organises seed collections; these seeds are then planted, germinated, and the saplings looked after for several years before being planted out.

Seeds can be collected by anyone as soon as they ripen, although it is far easier to wait until they drop to the ground. Because they must be fertile, it is best to collect where there is a group of trees. Native trees are most likely to be found in the countryside on ground that has remained untouched. To carry your seeds, use a hessian or open mesh bag or an open basket for larger seeds such as acorn. Avoid using plastic bags, as the seeds cannot breathe in them. After collection, some seeds can be planted immediately, while others will need a period of storage in a cool, dark place to prepare them for germination. This process is called 'stratification'.

Before planting a tree in your garden, think about how much space it will need and the effect it will have on the rest of your garden. Will it be greedy, sucking all the goodness out of the soil, like the silver birch with its roots close to the surface? Will it be possible to plant right up to its base as you can with apple and pear trees? What kind of root system does it have? As a general rule, the roots will mirror the spread of the branches above. If a long-established tree hogs moisture from the soil in your garden, add manure and mulches at least twice a year to the affected area.

Some Native Trees (Ireland and Britain)

ALDER: In ancient times, the trunks of this traditional tree were used for making shields. Gather the ripe cones in autumn and when they have dried out, shake them into a container to release the seeds.

BIRCHES (silver): The silver birch can make a good ornamental tree for a housing estate as it does not grow too large. Gather the blooms, or 'catkins', when they are dry. These will fall apart, releasing the seeds.

HAZEL: Hazelnuts were associated with some of the very earliest human settlers on this planet and the wood is still used for fencing and wattling. The nuts can be collected directly from the trees when they turn brown.

OAK: The finest of trees, the wood of the oak has been highly regarded down the centuries. When the acorns turn brown, they will fall to earth where they can be collected.

Growing Your Own

So what about your own garden? Trees in your garden will provide structure and focus, as well as privacy and a windbreak. They will help suppress weeds and can be used to screen out an ugly shed or view. In summer, trees provide height, colour and fragrance. In winter, their bark can be as beautiful as any foliage or flower.

Trees have the huge virtue of being trouble-free after the initial year or so. Once fully established, there is little work involved. Unlike flowers, vegetables and some shrubs, they do not need constant feeding, watering, pruning, spraying, staking and deadheading.

A tree is as close to a permanent structure as you will get in your garden and, after a few years, there will be no shifting it easily. So think hard before you plant a tree. Walk around the neighbourhood and look at what other people have done. Observe the size of the species they have planted. Go to parks and gardens and have a good look at the trees planted there. Reflect hard on how big a tree you want – a cute little sapling can grow into an overbearing giant inside a couple of decades.

Before you buy anything, find out how high it will grow in, say, ten years and then, for the sake of the neighbourhood, in fifty years. Even if your garden is small, the good news is that nature has provided us with such a range of trees, from giant oaks and firs to tiny bonsais, that everyone can grow one of their own. So do your research and draw up a short-list.

At the garden centre, check carefully before you buy. Test for general health by gently attempting to pull the young tree from its container. If it comes out easily, the plant is not well established. If roots are sprouting through the bottom, it has been there too long. Check for healthy leaves and strong stems growing in all directions. There should be no signs of pruning, indicating that the plant has been cut back. Do not be put off by a few small weeds or algae in the soil. This shows the plant is growing happily.

Before planting a tree, some preparation is required. Dig deep to break up not only the topsoil but also the next layer, and fork in plenty of manure or compost. Add a balanced fertilizer, following the instructions of the manufacturer. Water the plant thoroughly by putting it in a bucket of water and soaking it for a few hours. Then, if it came in a container, remove this carefully and tease out tangled roots without breaking up the soil ball. Make sure the base of the plant's stem is slightly below the surface when it comes to filling in the hole. Once the tree is planted, firm everything by treading down the ground around the base of the plant, and water thoroughly.

Your first choice could be a fruit tree. Or you may take an interest in a particular species such as Japanese maples. Certain shrubs can grow large and tree-like. There is a huge choice; here are some ideas.

Fruit Trees

APPLE: The apple tree is certainly native to the northern European climate, but can be unpredictable, especially if sited in a cold spot, as it needs sun to produce blossoms and fruit. Apple trees are also prone to disease, most notably mildew, and in the first four years will need careful feeding, mulching and pruning. A lot will depend on the quality of the specimen you buy but, unfortunately, you may not know how hardy this is until after a few heart-breaking years. There are literally hundreds of varieties of apple tree. Some grow to about 10.5m (34ft) and should be avoided by the suburban gardener, especially since dwarf varieties can be grown in a large pot, while others can be trained against a wall. Most apple trees will need a similar tree nearby for pollination. Ask lots of questions before you buy.

CHERRY: The modern cherry tree grows only to about 6m (20ft) and is self-pollinating. Needing only a sunny position and protection from birds, it is a good choice for the fledgling gardener as it will produce fruit in its first year. The most popular variety is morello, with pretty white blossoms in spring and fruit ready for picking in August.

FIG: Fig trees are readily available in garden centres and are easy to grow, though in need of a lot of attention. Any soil will do and spraying is not necessary. The best place to grow a fig tree is against a south-facing wall. When planting, restrict the root growth by keeping it in a pot before putting it in the ground. In winter, cover embryo fruits and young shoots individually to protect them from frost. Even after all that trouble, it is still difficult to get a fig tree to fruit.

PEAR: Although closely related to the apple, the pear tree is more temperamental, hating the cold and unlikely to flourish in sandy or chalky soil. It is slower to come into fruit, taking anything up to eight years, and the yield will be lower. Only one or two varieties will self-pollinate so you will need to grow two trees. But although not as hardy, a thriving pear tree can live for over a century – about twice the life span of the average apple tree.

PLUM: A plum tree may not be top of everyone's list but can be easy to grow and indeed can reach heights of 6m (20ft) when mature. It blossoms early and is best planted on a high spot for a good crop. Silver-leaf disease is a constant threat, while netting may be needed to keep off birds, who target the buds in spring and the fruit later on. Judicious pruning should be done between June and late July, and never in winter.

QUINCE: This is worth growing in warmer areas for its gnarled and contorted trunk and branches, grey bark and attractive dark green leaves. It produces blossoms in June and fruit in October. During the first few years, a quince will need pruning. It will grow to about 3.6m (12ft).

An A-Z of Other Trees

Deciduous

ALDER (*Alnus*): A fast grower, the tallest of the species is the Italian alder or *A. cordata*, with glistening leaves and large 'cones'. A smaller variety is the golden-leaf alder (*A. glutinosa* 'Aurea'), with pale yellow leaves, which grows to about 3.6m (12ft). Alders are not suitable for chalky soils.

ASH (*Fraxinus*): The common ash tree is one for the large estate or park, with an invasive root system and a likely height of 18m (60ft). Of the smaller varieties, none is particularly attractive, but 'Jaspidea' will turn into a 4.5m (15ft) tree with yellow branches and foliage.

BEECH (*Fagus*): Best used as a hedge, this is a huge tree that grows to 30m (100ft) and higher, and needs lots of space.

BIRCH (*Betula*): The familiar silver birch (*B. pendula*), with its yellowish catkins and peeling bark, will grow to about 10.7m (35ft). It is not a difficult tree to grow, being very hardy and thriving in most soils, though it will need watering in a drought, because its roots do not go very deep.

CHERRY BLOSSOM (*Prunus*): This is another one everyone knows, a welcome sight on our streets at the end of winter. Typically, cherry blossoms grow to 6m (20ft) and will flower between March and May. There are all kinds of varieties and also a number of related species such as ornamental almonds, plums and peaches. They will flourish in most soils and like a trace of lime.

ELM (*Ulmus*): The elm came to everyone's attention with the disastrous outbreak of Dutch elm disease some decades ago. Very few are left in our parks but mature varieties can reach over 30m (100ft) in height. The most disease-resistant variety is the Chinese elm (*U. parvifolia*), growing to 12m (40ft) and with glossy green leaves that remain until late December.

EUCALYPTUS: The eucalyptus, or gum tree, with its waxy blue leaves, grows rapidly and must be pruned back in spring; otherwise it will grow to heights of about 15m (50ft).

FLOWERING CRAB (*Malus sylvestris*): This one is often confused with the cherry blossom, producing pink and red blossom in the spring and heralding the arrival of summer. The crab-apple is also used for making a traditional jam or jelly.

HAWTHORN (*Crataegus*): A common sight in hedgerows, the hawthorn is an excellent specimen tree for a lawn, growing to 4.5m (15ft), and can also be used as a hedge. Being a native of northern Europe, it is not fussy about either soil or weather conditions, and will produce its characteristic reddish blossoms in spring and its distinctive red berries or 'haws' in autumn whatever the conditions.

HAZEL (*Corylus*): The hazel tree, with its many stems, produces yellow catkins in February or March and is known mainly for its nuts. The common hazel, *C. avellana*, will grow to about 3m (10ft), while *C. colurna* will reach heights three times that. There are also more decorative varieties, such as *C. avellana* 'Contorta', also known as the 'corkscrew hazel' or, irresistibly, 'Harry Lauder's Walking Stick'. With its curious twisting branches, this one grows slowly to about 2.4m (8ft).

HORSE CHESTNUT (*Aesculus*): The horse chestnut comes in a number of varieties, the common horse chestnut (*A. hippocastanum*) growing to a gigantic 24m (80ft). To grow, just plant one of the 'conkers' that fall from the tree in autumn. There is also a more modest variety, the *A. pavia*, that grows no more than 3m (10ft).

JAPANESE ACER: In Japan, the acer or maple has long been admired and it features not only in the country's

Japanese Acers are good in containers

ornamental gardens but also in its poetry and art. The result is
that there are now over 300 varieties of Japanese acer. In these
parts, the most common (and cheapest) are the *A. palmatum*
and the *A. japonicum*. Go to any well-stocked garden centre
and you will find a variety of these trees at different stages of
growth. The leaves come in many colours, though yellow and
wine-red are the most usual, while the foliage can range from
narrow fern-like fringes to broader, though still delicate, leaves.
This is a tree you could get hooked on, but shop around before
buying, as prices can vary enormously.

LABURNUM: This graceful tree with its hanging sprays of
yellow flowers can add an elegant touch to the front lawn and
will grow to about 4.5m (15ft). Following the flowers are long
brown pods and shiny green leaves. The twigs, leaves and
especially the seeds of the laburnum are highly poisonous.

LIME (*Tilia*): Lime or linden trees, with their heart shaped
leaves, grow to over 30m (100ft) in height, dwarfing even the
oak and beech. So they are best left in the park, where their tiny
fragrant flowers can be admired.

MAPLE (*Acer*): The ordinary sycamore (*A. pseudo-
plantanus*) is the best-known member of this family, prolifically

self-seeding and growing to 9m (30ft) or so very quickly. The field maple (*A. campestre*) is a native northern European tree, growing to about 6m (20ft). There are other varieties with more interesting foliage and barks (see Japanese acer above).

MOUNTAIN ASH (*Sorbus*): This graceful and slender tree provides colour all year round, with blossoms in spring and leaves and berries later on. The rowan, with its red berries, is part of this family. The closely related whitebeams include the 3m (10ft) tall *S.hostii*, which is suitable for small gardens. Other varieties grow considerably taller.

OAK (*Quercus*): Another tree best suited to the park. All oaks are imposing and the red oak will grow to 24m (78ft) and produce vivid red leaves in autumn if grown in acid soil. These are among the longest-living and most majestic of trees.

PALMS: In their native habitat, palms grow into huge trees, many exceeding 30m (100ft) in height. In colder climates, they stay much smaller, but still add a touch of the tropical to our gardens. Choose your palm carefully, as not all will survive a harsh winter. Best choice is the Chinese windmill palm (*Trachycarpus fortunei*), with large fan-like leaves and those strange white puffballs in a mild summer.

PLANE (*Platanus*): Not one for the garden, growing to 24m (80ft), but great for soaking up pollution in an urban park.

POPLAR (*Populus*): In the wrong place, the poplar can topple a building. Its roots will damage drains, raise paving stones on footpaths and undermine the foundations of a house. This is a tree that demands open spaces, as it soars to a height of 24m (80ft) in just twenty years. No wonder it is used so widely as a practical and eye-catching windbreak on European roads.

WALNUT (*Juglans*): The walnut can turn into another 30m (100ft) monster in a sheltered site. Nuts appear about ten years after planting.

WILLOW (*Salix*): In its rightful place beside a pond, a weeping willow is a magnificent sight; the back garden is rarely the place for this graceful and fast-growing tree. Choose instead one of the more compact versions of willow, such as the American weeping willow (*S. purpurea 'Pendula'*), which grows to 4.5m (15ft) and has purple-tinged branches. Or there is the Kilmarnock willow (*S. caprea 'Pendula'*) with its distinctive 'pussy willow' catkins. Of the non-weeping varieties of willow, the corkscrew (*S. matsudana 'Tortuosa'*) develops twisted and contorted branches and rises to over 7.5m (25ft) in height.

Conifers

Almost all conifers are evergreen and most come with needle-like leaves. Even the exceptions, such as ginkgo, produce cones. While magnificent in a park or large formal garden, standard conifers are rarely suitable for the ordinary suburban garden, especially as their eventual height is difficult to predict. Some varieties can grow slowly for their first 30 years and then put on a huge spurt. Dwarf varieties, though, are very useful for plugging a hole in the border, or as specimen trees. In recent years, some varieties, such as false cypress, have become popular for making hedges. Though not quite as dull as griselinia, these are still a bit uninspiring, so use with discretion.

CALIFORNIAN REDWOOD (*Sequoia*): This is the oldest and biggest tree in the world. Some are thought to be over 1200 years old and one specimen in the USA is the world's tallest tree at 110m (366ft). Obviously not a species that will suit the average garden, but dwarf versions can be found.

CEDAR: The magnificent cedar belongs in a public space where it can be truly appreciated. The much-loved cedar of Lebanon, for instance, will grow to 24m (80ft) or more, as will the drooping deodara and the blue cedar. Dwarf versions are available, but choose with care.

CYPRESS (*Cupressus*): Coming from the warmer parts of Europe, the cypress does not travel well and has long been surpassed by the false cypress as a utility tree.

FALSE CYPRESS (*Chamaecyparis*): You will find a huge range from this family of trees in any garden centre. There are miniature versions for the rockery, dwarfs for the small garden, and larger examples that can be used for hedges or individually as a showpiece in a large lawn. Unlike the true cypress, the cones are small and the plants are hardier, although they prefer a sheltered site and well-drained soil.

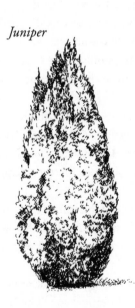

Juniper

JUNIPER: This is a ground-hugging conifer, long popular in the USA. There are many varieties, all of them hardy and tolerant both of poor conditions and regular pruning. They all have a berry-like cone. An ideal specimen plant for a small garden is *J. virginiana* 'Skyrocket', a narrow, slim tree that will grow to about 1.8m (6ft) in ten years and about 4.5m (15ft) when fully grown.

LARCH (*Larix*): One of the few conifers to lose its leaves during winter. A fast-growing forestry tree not suitable for the garden.

LEYLAND CYPRESS (*Cupressocyparis leylandii*): The most popular conifer for hedges, *leylandii* withstands heavy pruning, is hardy and grows about 1.20m (4ft) a year, faster than any other conifer. But it is not suitable for all locations, as even a single example needs plenty of space.

MAIDENHAIR (*Ginkgo*): The ginkgo comes in a single species that goes back about 200 million years in time. It does not look a conifer, with its fan-shaped leaves turning yellow and falling off in autumn. Rather than a cone, it occasionally produces a small yellow fruit, widely used in herbal medicine for its positive effect on the memory. It will reach heights of about 18m (60ft).

MONKEY PUZZLE (*Araucaria*): This distinctive tree with its skyward-pointing stems became something of a craze in Victorian times. It grows slowly at first but will end up an imposing 20m (70ft) or so. Not one for the small garden.

PINE (*Pinus*): The tall Scots pine is native to these parts and, with its long narrow needles, many would feel that it is a far more attractive tree than the more popular false cypresses, junipers and spruces. Dwarf versions are available, but may not be easy to find.

SILVER FIR (*Abies*): In the open, the silver fir will grow to 30m (100ft). A slow-growing dwarf version, *A. balsamea* 'Hudsonia', is useful for rock gardens, while *A. arizonica* 'Compacta', growing to less than 2.20m (7ft), is suitable for the average garden.

SPRUCE (*Picea*): As the standard Christmas tree, the spruce is bought by the million every winter and then thrown out. It is the most important timber tree in Europe, with its wood sold everywhere as 'white deal'.

YEW (*Taxus*): This slow-growing conifer is tolerant of poor air and shade when it is planted in well-drained soil. The Irish yew, in both its green and yellow versions, will grow no higher than 4.5m (15ft), a rate of about 1.5m (5ft) every ten years.

The common yew, growing to 12m (40ft), is a familiar sight in churchyards.

Six Trees for Small Gardens

- *Acer negundo* 'Flamingo'
- Crab apple 'Red Sentinel'
- Hawthorn 'Rosea Flore Pleno'
- Japanese maple 'Osakazuki'
- *Laburnum x wateri* 'Vossii'
- Willow 'Hakuro-nishiki'

9. Flowers Everywhere

Most gardeners begin their career by buying a few plants and flowers from the local gardening centre, digging a hole, and sticking them in the ground without much in the way of deep thinking. 'Real' gardeners may get snooty about this, but how else is the novice to learn? By watching how a plant reacts to light, shade, wetness or dryness; by seeing how much it grows in a year and for how long it blooms, new gardeners will absorb much and develop their own tastes in flowers and plants. What's the harm in that?

The dictionary describes a flower as 'a bloom or blossom on a plant' or 'a plant that bears blooms and blossoms'. What it does not say is that there are thousands of varieties of flowers and that the novice gardener can be forgiven for feeling bewildered. What, for instance, is the difference between a shrub and a flower? Shrubs flower, don't they? This is not too hard a question to answer: flowers have soft stems that are easy to cut with a scissors, while shrubs have woody stems that will need clipping. You would not usually be inclined to snip off their blooms for an indoor display, however beautiful they may be.

For most of us, the first thing we notice about a flower is its colour and, after that, its size and personality. A stroll through the gardening centre reveals all kinds of other classifications. There are annuals, perennials and biennials. There are plants that grow from bulbs and others that spring from seeds. Some plants prefer acid soil while others like alkaline, or more chalky soil, rich in lime. Then there is the time of year when they will bloom, another potential minefield. In the ideal garden, we are supposed to have something blooming every month of the year. For novices, getting anything to bloom at any time is a major source of satisfaction.

It is best to start small. Buy anything you find attractive and plant carefully according to the instructions. After that, water regularly and watch. You may find that you do not really like roses, or gladioli, or nasturtiums. You will see that certain plants do not thrive in your garden, or are too susceptible to slugs. You will probably realise that mixing up flowers and shrubs of varying heights is a good idea. With growing confidence, you will start buying several rather than just one of a flower you like. You will learn to take cuttings of favourites as the year progresses and perhaps even grow some from seed. Before you know where you are, you will be a true gardener!

Beginner's Bulbs

The novice gardener can get a lot of pleasure from planting bulbs. For most people, flowers in the garden mean a display of snowdrops followed by daffodils and crocuses in the spring and then tulips right through until June. All grow from bulbs and because they are so universally popular, they can be bought anywhere, from garden centres to supermarkets. Buy them in the autumn and get them into the ground before the earth freezes up for winter. That's all there is to it – no fiddling with seed beds and propagators and no laborious planting-out routines. It could not be easier.

Buying bulbs is an investment, as most of your plants are

certain to increase in numbers over the years, being prolific self-seeders after they bloom. So it is worth taking a little trouble with them. Buy good quality bulbs, sow them in clumps at the right time, and when planting, put a little bone meal in the bottom of each hole before popping them in.

Bulb

The term 'bulb' is used here to cover the entire range of bulbous plants, encompassing corms, rhizomes and tubers as well as bulbs. Although all store food for the plant inside themselves, they are quite different botanically. A true bulb, such as a tulip or narcissus (generic term for all varieties of daffodil), is a specialised shoot with the swollen leaves or scales lightly folded over each other. It looks like an onion. The corm is one solid, swollen stem; a rhizome is a fleshy stem that creeps under the earth's surface; while a root tuber is a looser form of bulb.

Rhizome

For a Spring Show

Sow all these in mid- to late-autumn.

CROCUS: There are hundreds of crocuses, ranging from the smaller, early varieties, which can flower from mid-January, to the more familiar big Dutch types, which flower at the same time as daffodils, but are by no means as long-lasting, and are susceptible to the strong winds of March. After their short flowering period, they quickly fade away, leaving no trace. For making clumps, go for the yellow-brown blooms of

C. chrysanthus 'E.P. Bowles' or similar. These can be planted in grass, because the leaves do not last too long.

DAFFODILS AND NARCISSI: Daffodils and narcissi both belong to the *narcissus* family, and while all varieties are yellow, they can look quite different, the daffodil having the longer and larger 'trumpet'. Since the various species and varieties come out at different times of the season, plant about a dozen of the same variety in a clump so that they all bloom together. Early varieties are best left in the ground to increase over the years and will do particularly well under trees. Miniatures are also widely available and are well worth trying; mix them up with some early blue anemones (*A. appenina* or *A. blanda*) for an eye-catching display. Try planting in grass (the official term is 'naturalising'), though their foliage can make mowing the lawn awkward at a crucial time of the year. If you put in just one or two, simply mow over them.

GRAPE HYACINTH (*Muscari*): With their deep blue spikes of flowers, the grape hyacinth is a welcome addition to the spring garden, blooming around the same time as daffodils. Most varieties are hardy and spread rapidly.

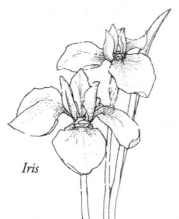

Iris

IRIS RETICULATA: The most popular and reliable iris for winter planting, *Iris reticulata* varieties such as 'Harmony' and 'Joyce' produce blue flowers from late January and flourish in any sheltered position in full sun. There are also yellow, white and violet varieties.

Snowdrops

SNOWDROPS: Pick a sheltered spot for your snow-drops under a tree or hedges. They start appearing in January and, after a few years, a dozen or so will have become a thick carpet. To plant, either dig a small hole for each, or simply scatter them on the surface, rake them in and cover with a thin layer of compost. Buy plenty, since not all will flourish, and lift and divide every couple of years. There is an argument that snowdrops are best bought and planted in spring.

TULIPS: Tulips can require lifting, drying off and replanting, which sounds like altogether too much bother unless you are a tulip fanatic. But if you put a group of six to fifteen in the spaces between shrubs and perennials, they can be left pretty much alone and will flower for a few seasons at least. Tulips can vary in size, from a few centimetres to 1m (3ft) in height, and also come with the greatest range of colours in the flower world. It is a flower that has inspired mania in collectors – after the first wild tulip was introduced from Turkey to Holland in the 17th century, enthusiasts went completely mad, quite happy to re-mortgage their houses for a single bulb. Unfortunately, the original bulbs suffered from a virus that caused streaks and featherings of a different colour and led to the so-called 'broken' tulip strands. The parrot tulip comes from this strand, with big flowers and strange colourings. These are best grown alone. The most reliable tulips are the single-earlies and the tall Darwin types. Since they are not dependable for a second season if left in the ground, they need lifting for the winter. Snap off the heads as soon as flowering is over, and then dig them up just before the foliage has completely died down. Store them over the summer and replant in the autumn, maybe in combination with wallflowers.

Summer Bulbs

Spring-planted bulbs will flower a few months later. Gladioli, hyacinths and lilies are probably the most common.

ANEMONES: A packet of bulbs (or rather tubers) planted in spring will brighten up the border from June to September. Anemones come in a variety of cheerful colours and styles.

GLADIOLI: Although these flowers have become something of a joke, they are particularly good value if you like them. Each corm you plant in spring will have become two by the time you come to lift them in autumn for winter storage. 'Glads' can add a splash of colour to a vegetable patch and come in a wide variety, including more discreet miniatures.

HYACINTHS: The summer hyacinth is particularly worth buying. With its delicate white bells on long stems that flower from August, it is the perfect plant to mix in with low-lying ground cover or smaller bedding plants. It grows best from bulblets.

LILIES: Most lilies flower in June and July, adding welcome colour to the summer garden. They are the ideal flower to put between shrubs, which they will use as a prop, not being strong enough to stand on their own. Lilies like moist but well-drained soil and prefer to keep their heads in the sun and their roots well-shaded. Put them down no deeper than 10cms (4ins) in September. To multiply your supply of bulbs, strip several of the outer scales from a bulb you have either bought or dug up, put in a plastic bag of soil-less compost, and hang at a window. After about three weeks, roots will show and, when these are long enough, put each new little plant in a separate pot.

Autumn Bulbs

Bulbs put down in July or even early August will flower a month or so later. The **autumn crocus** is the most common, along with **colchicum**, often confused with the true crocus. The difference lies in their development underground. True crocuses have corms that last only a year, leaving behind 'offsets' that will flower the next season. By contrast, the colchicum grows directly from the original bulb each year and this should be lifted and divided. Crocuses are best planted in a spot where they will not become a nuisance as they spread. Choose a sheltered patch where the grass does not grow too vigorously. Ideally, colchicums should be put among shrubs, as they need richer soil and prefer some shade.

Another autumn-flowering bulb is the **cyclamen**, a beautiful low-growing plant with elegant white or pink flowers, which, although a tuber, is best bought in a pot. Gaining popularity as autumns become warmer is the tall and startlingly pink **nerine** with its large bulb peeping out of the soil.

Annuals

Annuals, or bedding plants, are invaluable for the occasional gardener. Usually sold in trays, they add instant colour and life to borders at any time of the year, making them difficult to resist. When they die, you simply dig them up and get in more, or if you are really adventurous, and have space for seed trays indoors, you can start growing them yourself. Annuals give you the ideal opportunity to experiment, as whatever you do will last for only a few months. Different varieties have different needs. Hardy annuals, such as the Californian poppy, cornflower and love-in-a-mist, can be sown in late summer for the following season. Half-hardy annuals that will bloom later in the season can be sown in spring in seed trays and require careful attention before being transferred to their eventual location. Just because they last for only one season does not mean that they will not grow big, so give your annuals plenty of space. Remember also to water them frequently; all flowering plants tend to be very thirsty.

What follows is a guide to some of the more popular annuals. Check them out in your local garden centre. Most come in a variety of colours.

AFRICAN DAISY (*Osteospernum*): With large, daisy-like flowers in an assortment of colours, this compact plant, growing to about 30cms (1ft), needs the sun, since the flowers will not open on a dull day. Buy just one plant and then break off pieces from close to the bottom; they will take root wherever you stick them in the ground.

ALYSSUM: What would a flowerbed be without the single row of alyssum fringing it to the front? Some might say that this is reason enough to ignore this useful plant which can be used in all sort of places. 'Snow drift' is a white variety, while 'Royal Carpet' is red.

BEGONIA: Few plants can match the begonia for its range of colours. The rose-like *B. tuberhybrida* are the most popular of the many varieties available and have a double bloom, with the small female one hiding under the more flamboyant male. This should be pinched out. Begonias are best planted as tubers in early spring or bought in from June, as they are difficult to raise from seed. For bright red, go for the 'Non-Stop Rose' variety. 'Midas' is yellow, while 'Diana Wynyard' is white. All begonias are good value, will last the entire summer and are relatively slug-resistant.

BUSY LIZZIE (*Impatiens*): This popular house plant moved outdoors only after new hardy hybrids such as 'Super Elfin' and 'Accent' were developed, proving a gift for gardeners seeking summer colour in awkward spots, such as under trees. New varieties and colours are continually being added to the busy lizzie collection, making it one of the top ten most popular bedding plants.

CANTERBURY BELLS (*Campanula*): This traditional cottage garden plant produces high spikes of white, blue or even pink bells, depending on the variety. *C. pyramidalis* 'Chimney' is a spectacular giant that will need staking, while 'Stella' is good for hanging baskets.

CARNATION: Another flower that comes in many colours, carnations will bloom happily all summer. Among the many red varieties is the tall 'Scarlet Luminette' that, happily, does not need staking. 'Knight mixed' is a popular dwarf in many colours.

CHRYSANTHEMUM: Deservedly popular and easy to grow, chrysanthemums come in many shapes and sizes. 'Court Jesters' and 'Merry Mixture' produce spectacular flowers with rings of red, yellow and white. Go for 'Gold Plate' as a bright yellow edging plant, or choose the perennial 'Marguerite', usually grown as an annual, for a simple, white flower.

CINERARIA: With its silver leaves, cineraria can provide a subtle backdrop for more extrovert annuals, like salvia or begonia. Although cineraria produces small yellow flowers, these should be removed at the budding stage if the plant is grown simply for its foliage. It prefers a warm spot with well-drained soil.

DAHLIA: The more popular varieties of dahlia, a half-hardy perennial, produce plate-sized blooms. The bedding version of dahlia does not grow quite as large but is less trouble and easily raised from seed, providing a colourful show from July on. The standard dahlia is the 'Coltness Gem Hybrid', producing large single flowers. The more unusual 'Dandy' has small narrow petals backed by a fringe of larger petals. Dahlias need some attention. Dig in plenty of manure before planting and water and feed regularly during the season.

FORGET-ME-NOT (*Myosotis*): Traditionally found under a bed of tulips, the blue varieties of forget-me-not, such as 'Ultramarine' and 'Blue Ball', are great favourites, but white and pink versions are also available.

FOXGLOVE (*Digitalis*): With its tall spires of bell-like flowers, this is another old favourite that still grows in the wild and has a long blooming period. A variety such as 'Sutton's Abricot' comes in a nice soft pink. A biennial treated as an annual that can be grown from seed.

HIBISCUS: The development of an assortment of hybrids means that the hibiscus is no longer just a houseplant but comes in large, medium and dwarf varieties that can serve as bedding or as an eye-catching individual plant. The exotic 'Dixie Belle' is worth trying in a warm, shady spot.

LOBELIA: Usually coming in blue, lobelia joins alyssum as the edging flower of choice for thousands of gardeners, with 'Mrs Clibran Improved' a well-established favourite. Clip off the tips of plants after the first flowering. They are easy to grow from their tiny dust-like seeds, but even easier to buy in trays.

LOVE-IN-A-MIST (*Nigella*): With its flowers peeping through delicate, silky foliage, this slightly old-fashioned flower is aptly named. Originally blue in colour, the 'Persian Jewels' variety offers whites, pinks and purples. *Nigella* is easy to grow and will flower for about six weeks after its first show in June.

MARIGOLDS: If you want the colours yellow or orange for your flowerbed, the much-loved marigold is sure to be your first choice. Marigolds are easy to grow from seed; they are cheap, very hardy and will flower from June until October. French marigold varieties produce lots of single and double blooms; the African marigold is a bit taller and can produce larger blooms, while the French-African hybrids take the best characteristics of the parent varieties. If buying in trays, plant out before the flowers open and if some of the buds have opened, snap them off. Protect your marigolds from slugs and, in all but the hybrids, deadhead to prolong flowering.

NASTURTIUM: A great favourite with children for its easy-growing qualities, the red, yellow and orange nasturtium comes in climbing, semi-trailing and bedding varieties. 'Whirlybird' is one of the best of the dwarf varieties.

NICOTIANA: Worth planting for its scent, the standard nicotiana, or tobacco plant, produces clusters of yellowish-white flowers that can add subtlety to the flowerbed. A perennial treated as a half-hardy annual, it can be grown easily from seed. The original *N. alata*, with its blooms opening only in the evening, has the most intense scent, while *N. sylvestris* is an award-winning variety.

PANSY: If you are looking for a flower that will provide colour all year round, then the pansy is the answer to your prayers. This small and versatile bedding plant comes in all the colours of the rainbow, with the exception of green. Closely related to violas, pansies are taller and less compact. Faced varieties have a black marking or 'face' at the centre of the bloom; bi-coloured types come in two colours, usually white and something else, while there are also plain, single-coloured varieties. Deadhead regularly, water, and protect from slugs.

PELARGONIUM: Often (and mistakenly) described as geraniums, these are the standard plant for window-boxes and hanging baskets, as they do not need constant watering. There are four types: 'ivy leafed' has attractive trailing foliage, 'regal' has large richly coloured flowers, 'scented leaved' has aromatic foliage, and 'zonal' has leaves with a band of a different colour running through them. The 'Breakaway' varieties were developed for containers, although it is the ivy-leafed types like 'Red Mini Cascade' that are the true trailers. Bedding varieties include 'Pandora' and 'Mrs Lawrence'. All pelargoniums are easy to grow and a cheering addition to any garden.

PETUNIA: Another great favourite for hanging baskets and containers, petunias come in a wide variety of colours and styles, from the standard funnel-shaped blooms to more puffball types. The 'Multifloras' are best as bedding plants, while the 'Cascade' series is suitable for hanging baskets.

POLYANTHUS: Like the pansy, polyanthus is usually bought by the dozen in trays as a handy bedding staple that flowers in March and again in the autumn. Preferring shade, it

Poppy

needs protection from birds and slugs. A cross between the primrose and the cowslip, polyanthus can be grown from seed, but why bother when it is so widely available, even in the depths of winter?

POPPY (*Papaver*): What can be more eye-catching than a poppy? The 'Shirley' poppies are the ones to buy for bedding, while 'Mother of Pearl' comes in unusual pastel colours. Iceland poppies are smaller, with bright yellow or red flowers. The annuals are best sown where they will flower, as they do not like transplanting. The only problem

121

with poppies is that the blooms, after they arrive, last only a day or two. The pods contain hundreds of seeds that can be kept for the following year or used in baking as decoration on bread.

POT MARIGOLD (*Calendula*): This bushy, fast-growing plant is easy to grow in any well-drained soil, but needs diligent deadheading to keep it going over the summer. It will tolerate partial shade. The most popular bush variety is the 'Fiesta Gitana', an ideal edging plant. Other varieties, such as 'Art Shades', are taller.

PRIMROSE (*Primula*): The common primrose in its pale yellow livery is a standard wild garden flower. If you do not mind it coming in various shades of pink, there is also the 'Japanese' or 'Candelabra' primrose that grows about 60cms (2ft) high and is the easiest to raise from seed.

SALVIA SPLENDENS: A half-hardy perennial grown as an annual in any reasonable soil, the 'Scarlet Sage' variety of salvia produces attractive pillar-box red tubular flowers, which are often used as a cheap alternative to pelargoniums in colour schemes needing bright red. Salvias are not just red – there are blue, lilac and white varieties. They need protection from slugs.

SNOW CARPET (*Lobularia maritima*): This fast-growing annual with grey-green leaves and dozens of tiny, honey-scented flowers is ideal for ground cover.

STOCK: In the past, stock, with its small, thickly clustered spikes of flowers, and attractive grey-green foliage, was a mainstay of the formal bed. It is not so popular now, mainly because its flowering period is short and it is difficult to raise some varieties from seed. There are two main groups of stock: the 'Ten Week Stocks', sown in February, planted out in May and flowering in June, and the 'Brompton Stocks', biennials that are sown outdoors in May and pricked out for the winter, for flowering the following April. Then there is 'Night-Scented

Stock', a hardy annual sown in spring with a powerful fragrance at night.

SUNFLOWER (*Helianthus*): Growing to almost 3m (10ft) in height, the sunflower can be rather startling in the wrong position but, well-placed, is another cheerful addition to a border, though difficult enough to grow from seed. Try 'Sunburst' for more unusual markings – a red ring around the dark centre and yellow petals.

SWEET PEA (*Lathyrus odoratus*): One of the classics, producing a mass of blooms, sweet peas need a sunny, protected spot. To grow, the seeds should be sown in pots in autumn, then watered, covered with newspaper and left in a cool spot such as a porch, if a cold-frame or greenhouse is not available. When the seedlings emerge, remove the newspaper and leave them in the open, except in severely cold weather. Pinch out the top of the seedlings when they have produced two or three pairs of seeds. Move to the garden in late spring, spacing them about 20cms (8ins) apart. As they grow, each individual plant will need support. Do not allow to dry out in warm weather and deadhead regularly. The tall climbing sweet peas remain a favourite, trained up a trellis or netting or over a wigwam of canes. The popular 'Spencer' varieties provide a wide range of colours, from pale pink to dark purple. There are also hedge and dwarf varieties, and the carpeting 'Cupid', none of which require support.

SWEET WILLIAM (*Dianthus*): This short-lived perennial can be grown as a hardy biennial and produces heads of densely packed and sweetly scented flowers.

VERBENA: With both upright and spreading varieties, the small primrose-like verbena can be used as edging or in boxes and hanging baskets. It is slow to germinate from seeds but can be propagated by cuttings.

VIOLA: These small pansy-like perennials, grown as annuals, stay in bloom all summer and come in single plain colours or with dark blotches or lines from the centre.

WALLFLOWER (*Erysimum cheiri*): The sweetly scented wallflower, coming in all shades from white to deep purple, is a mainstay of the flowerbed in spring, rivalled only by tulips and daffodils. Wallflowers come in all sizes, from the dwarf 'Tom Thumb Mixed' to the 60cm (2ft) 'Double-flowered Branching Mixture'. Try 'Bowles Mauve', which is purple, or grow the small bush-like biennial 'Dwarf Prince Red' from seed. Cut back regularly and plants will continue to flower. Seeds are best sown in early summer and then planted out in autumn for the following year.

ZINNIA: Good for cut flowers, the zinnia has stiff, hairy leaves and produces flowers in a range of colours. There are two main types of zinnia: those with daisy-like blooms and those with the puff-ball heads more often associated with dahlias. They also come in tall and short varieties.

More Unusual Annuals

AGERATUM: The *A. houstonianum* variety is a low-lying flower with a powder-puff head that makes a particularly good edging plant.

CHINA ASTER (*Callistephus chinesis*): In a sheltered sunny spot, this produces heavy chrysanthemum-type flowers. Needs fertile soil.

DOUBLOON (*Tagetes erecta*): Puff-ball flowers that bloom all summer. Can grow up to 90cms (3ft).

POACHED EGG FLOWER (*Limnanthes douglasii*): A low-lying plant with delicate yellow flowers, a white fringing and finely cut leaves.

SILVER CUP (*Lavatera trimestris*): This hardy annual produces large glossy flowers in a sunny position. Grows to about 60cms (2ft).

SPIDER FLOWER (*Cleome*): With its strange, pink-and-white flowers, the appropriately named spider flower can add a touch of the exotic to your garden and is a useful gap-filler. It will flourish only in full sun and needs lots of watering. Sow in February for planting out in late May; it flowers a month later.

Perennials

The problem with annuals is that after sowing, transplanting, feeding and watering them for up to nine months of the year, you then have to dig them up, throw them away and start again. By contrast, perennials need the minimum of care to encourage them to make a repeat performance, not only the following season but for many seasons into the future, when they can be given new life by digging them up, dividing them and putting them into fresh soil.

Shrubs are perennial and many of them flower. Plants that come from bulbs are also perennial, although some require lifting if they are to bloom again. Grasses are perennial. What follows is a list of some names you may not have come across already. Be aware also that desirable perennials, such as camellias, delphiniums, non-bulbous irises, peonies, phlox, pelargoniums, penstemons, chrysanthemums, Michaelmas daisies, primulas, geraniums, carnations and pinks, hostas, begonias, African violets and hellebores, come in many shapes, sizes and colours, often with only the slightest similarity to each other. The following list is organised by height as it is always a good idea to put your tall plants to the back of a border and your clump-forming ones to the front.

Tall

DELPHINIUM 'Black Knight': This blue-flowered giant can grow to over 1m (4ft) and needs space, careful staking and a good, fertile soil. It is ideal for planting in front of a hedge or wall as a backdrop to the border. 'Black Knight' is one of the Pacific hybrid group of delphiniums, with large flowers. There is also the 'Elatum' group of tall hybrids for outdoor use, and the 'Belladonna' group of shorter, bushy plants. Cut back after flowering.

FOXTAIL LILY (*Eremurus*): A spectacular perennial that can be used as a single specimen or in a group, growing as high as 2.50m (8ft), with soaring spears of yellow, white, red and orange flowers.

LUPIN: The best-known of the lupins are the 'Russell' hybrids'. These tall plants, coming in all colours except green, will produce long stems with distinctive cartwheel leaves and flowers that can reach over 1m (4ft) in height from May. In theory, they are easy to grow from seed or cuttings, but, unfortunately, slugs love them.

ORNAMENTAL RHUBARB (*Rheum*): The large version of this plant can grow to a spectacular 1.80m (6ft), so it needs careful positioning. 'Astrosanguineum' has rich, dark-red leaves. There are also several smaller species, all with striking foliage. They need plenty of nourishment and will flower from June.

PHORMIUM: The best-known variety, the New Zealand flax, with its upright, sword-like leaves, forms a dense clump in no time and can reach a height of 2.8m (9ft), so place it carefully. A smaller version, *P. cookianum*, with pale- to dark-green leaves, is perhaps more suited to the small garden.

TREE MALLOW (*Lavertera*): Producing small, white

blooms, this plant needs staking and prefers well-drained soil. The 'Barnsley' variety will reach a height of about 1.80m (6ft); 'Rosea' is more commonly planted.

Medium

ACHILLEA: Growing to about 1.2m (4ft), *A. filipendulina* 'Gold Plate', also called yarrow, produces densely-packed, flat yellow flowers on fern-like foliage and may need staking. Plant in March in a sunny, dry position for flowering from June to August.

ARTEMISIA: A shrubby perennial with a lovely aromatic smell, the soft grey colour of this plant in most of its varieties means it has all kinds of uses. Grows to a height of 90cms and spreads even farther, but can be cut back hard.

ASTER or **MICHAELMAS DAISY**: Depending on the type, the aster can flower any time from spring to autumn and comes in a variety of colours. There are perennial and annual asters. Plant them in a sunny, airy position to avoid problems like mildew and they will grow prolifically until as late as November. They need cutting back, because they can become invasive.

ASTILBE: The delicate foliage and feathery flowers of the astilbe make it a favourite, although it can be temperamental and prefers a rich, moist soil and light shade. Plant beside a shrub for the best effect. Watch out for greenfly in mid-summer.

BELLFLOWER (*Campanula latifolia*): Among the best known of perennials, the *C. persicifolia*, or peach-leafed bellflower, comes in several attractive varieties. Deadhead regularly and cut back hard after flowering to keep in good condition. Clump-forming varieties, such as *C. cochleariifolia*

'Elizabeth Oliver' and *C. x haylodgensis* 'Plena', are invaluable as ground cover.

CATMINT (*Nepeta*): Looking like an undisciplined lavender, catmint will grow outwards and upwards to about 60cms (2ft) in a few weeks and is ideal for bare patches between slow-growing trees or shrubs. Mulch in autumn and cut back hard at the end of the winter. Propagate by division.

CHINESE LANTERN (*Physalis alkekengii*): After the first flush of small, insignificant white flowers come the fruits and then the large, red, lantern-shaped calyx, or outer flower. It prefers a non-acid soil with plenty of lime and needs winter protection.

COLUMBINE (*Aquilegia*): The 'McKana Hybrids' are large yellow and crimson flowers, with fern-like foliage on long, slender stems that are pretty but short-lived. Columbine is easy to raise from seed and, once planted, will seed itself freely.

EUPHORBIA: Often dismissed as invasive, there are still many desirable varieties of euphorbia or spurge, a plant distinguished by its small, round flowers and coloured bracts. 'Wulfenii' can grow to spectacular heights, *E.* 'Fireglow' comes in a wonderful red colour, while *E. amygdaloides* will tolerate shade. 'Clarice Howard', a low-growing alpine, has fine, copper-tinged foliage, but is hugely invasive and should be planted in a pot. Spurges are at their best in early summer but beware when handling, as all produce a milky sap that can be irritating. Propagate from cuttings or by division.

GARDEN CHRYSANTHEMUM: If you thought chrys-anthemums came in just the 'pot mum' variety, think again. This is the most versatile of flowers, with all sorts of varieties, most of them flowering well into the autumn and even winter. Other popular flowers, such as the wild marguerite or ox-eye daisy, come from this genus, although they flower earlier.

Chrysanthemums like sun and need protection from the cold in winter. They will grow and grow; the only problem once planted is remembering which are annual and which perennial.

HELLEBORE: The best-known species of hellebore is probably the Christmas rose (*H. niger*) which produces saucer-like flowers from December to March in subtle shades of pink, and off-white. *H. foetidus*, the stinking hellebore, has nodding, green flowers edged with purple, while *H. orientalis*, the Lenten Rose, includes varieties such as 'Ballard's Group' with dark, almost purple flowers. Stake them as they grow larger. Hellebores do best in half-shade and need some protection against frost. They prefer a rich, moist soil and, once established, will grow into a thick bush. Hellebores are greedy plants, so mulch well after flowering.

HEUCHERA: A superb ground cover plant with deep crimson foliage and dainty sprays of white flowers on slender stems appearing from early summer. Propagate by division.

HIMALAYAN POPPY: (*Meconopsis grandis*): With its striking blue flowers, this delicate plant may not bloom every year and, like all poppies, is not long-lasting. It needs an acid soil and can be grown from seed.

JAPANESE ANEMONE: This autumn-flowering plant comes in an assortment of colours and in several double-headed varieties. It is undemanding if you give it plenty of space and plant it in a semi-shaded position. Protect in winter.

PEONY (*Paeonia*): The peony, one of the true aristocrats of the garden, will outlive almost anything else you plant. All varieties need cosseting, and even in a warm, sheltered spot, will take a couple of seasons to get established. There are all sorts of desirable varieties, usually providing a lavish display of opulent white, pink or red blooms in early summer. Feed well in spring and mulch in autumn. If you develop a peony fetish, expect to pay big money for more unusual varieties. The tree peony is a flowering shrub.

PHLOX: Phlox comes in all colours and most varieties are good for at least ten years. They should be planted in April for May flowering, and then propagated by division.

SOLIDAGO: An excellent filler plant that tolerates some shade, its cheerful plumes of tiny yellow flowers look like frosting on the deep green foliage. Cut back hard in autumn since it can be invasive.

Small

AFRICAN LILY (*Agapanthus*): The tall stems of the African lily support bunches of fine-leafed blue or white flowers in late summer. The *A. campanulatus* variety grows no more than 75cms (30ins).

ASTRANTIA: This hard-working small plant produces a profusion of star-like flowers in midsummer. *A. major* 'Shaggy' has coarse cream and green leaves and pinkish-white flowers, while 'Hadspen Blood' produces deep-red blooms.

GERANIUM: The true geranium in one of its many hardy, herbaceous varieties is a worthwhile and versatile plant that can provide excellent ground cover in all conditions. The violet-coloured dusky cranesbill, for instance, likes shade, produces unusual dark-crimson flowers in July, and can be divided afterwards. The widely available 'Johnson's Blue' cheerfully grows anywhere. Cut back to encourage new growth, and propagate by division at the end of the summer.

HOSTA (*Hostaceae*): With its waxy green leaves and long-stemmed flowers, hosta is a favourite for the edge of a border, although some varieties grow very large. The foliage comes in a variety of subtle shades and will do best in shade. Left undisturbed for a few years, its creeping root system can provide excellent ground cover over a large area. The only problem is the slug, which regards the hosta as a four-star feast and can devour several overnight. Slug-resistant varieties of hosta have been developed; look out for 'Frances Williams' with its large, deep blue-green leaves, which are so tough that most slugs give up.

LAVENDER: The most common form of lavender is the 'Hidcote Blue', though there are dozens of other varieties available at reasonable prices from the garden centre. English varieties are tougher than their French cousins, but with global warming, the more exotic types may well survive better than you expect. Your lavender will not grow much in the first year but then should take off, producing fragrant spikes of pale purple flowers over its grey-green foliage. For the novice gardener, lavender is an ideal candidate for propagating by cuttings in autumn. As it gets older, lavender needs cutting back so that it does not flop out of shape.

LILY OF THE VALLEY (*Convallaria*): Native to woodlands and preferring moist, shaded areas, lily of the valley produces sprays of sweet-smelling white flowers. Plant in autumn for the following May; lift and divide every three or four years.

PINK (*Dianthus*): The perfumed pink, a close relative of the carnation, comes in many elegant varieties, some of them annual; others ideal for the rock garden. Fully hardy, the perennial varieties last for many years in an open sunny position. Among the desirable varieties is *D. superbus*, with its deeply fringed pink to purple flowers that continue well into autumn. They can be propagated by division, cuttings or layering.

PRIMULA: With hundreds of varieties to chose from, primulas are ideal for providing a show of colour in spring.

They come in all shades and are simplicity itself to grow, needing only a bit of shade and lots of watering. They can be moved around easily and propagated by division after flowering.

The Rose

Whether grown as a shrub or a perennial, the rose is, without question, the most loved and most popular flower of them all, though many gardeners will be happy to enjoy the roses in other people's gardens without bothering to grow them themselves. Others grow nothing else and risk seeing their entire garden wiped out if infected by a disease or pest. So perhaps the best tactic is to use a rose bush or two as part of your overall scheme. For the tentative and the unconvinced, miniature varieties are cheap to buy and require the least attention. A climber or a rambling variety might also be worth considering as this can provide an attractive covering for a wall or shed.

With so many to choose from, there is a rose for almost all gardens, though most roses prefer a reasonably rich, slightly acid soil and are unlikely to flourish in sandy or dry conditions. Check out the neighbourhood gardens to see what varieties are growing. The bad news is that almost all roses have thorns, making the necessary ritual of pruning a painful experience.

There are five classes of rose – hybrid tea, floribunda, miniature, climbers and ramblers. Hybrid tea roses are the most popular, coming in both bush and standard varieties. The flower stems are long and the single bloom on each is big and well-formed. These can reach heights of up to 1.5m (5ft) and produce flowers with up to 40 petals wrapped around the central cone. They come in a variety of reds, pinks and yellows.

Rather than just one bloom per stem, cluster-flowered, or floribunda, roses, have several, though the individual blooms are not as well formed. This type of rose is ideal for bedding. Miniature roses are used for edging in beds and as pot or tub plants. They grow no higher than 45cms (18ins) and have smaller leaves and flowers.

Roses tied to a support can be made to climb; the ramblers have long pliable stems and produce one annual display of small flowers. Climbers, with stiff stems, have larger blooms and may flower a couple of times. Finally, shrub roses are taller than bedding roses.

From this short account, you will see that there is much to learn about roses. If you think they will become your passion, plant one and see how it works out. If you are still fascinated, acquire one of the many specialist books on the subject from your local library or bookshop.

Grasses and Ferns

Grasses, along with sedges and rushes, have grown in popularity as useful space fillers, but can be overdone. The tall pampas grass, with its feathery plumes, has become a bit too familiar (and can only be removed by burning if you get fed up with it), and what can be duller than a border filled with nothing but grasses and heathers in an effort to make it labour-free?

Most ornamental grasses need well-drained soil and plenty of sun, even those with their origins in temperate climates. There are some beautiful specimens in the better class of garden centre, but they can be very expensive. Still, varieties such as the golden-coloured *carex elata*, which grow to about 1m (3ft), are relatively cheap and can brighten up a border.

Festucas such as *F. amethystina* form low tufts of steel blue, needle-like leaves and are useful for filling in spaces. Perennial grasses are propagated by division and can bear cutting back in late autumn. A number of grasses produce attractive flower heads that can be dried for ornamental use.

Ferns, associated with damp conditions in north European woods, are usually planted for their foliage. The smaller types are perfect for a rock garden, while varieties such as the evergreen *Davallia fejeensis* are used in hanging baskets. Tropical ferns are best kept indoors as houseplants.

The Rock Garden

Small, compact plants that thrive on special rocky beds are called 'alpines', and though not all come from the high mountains, these perennials are all able to withstand huge variations in temperature. If you like them, why not build a special rockery or raised bed? It does not need to be too big and can act as a focal point in the garden. A warm, sunny spot is vital – alpines need good drainage and plenty of sunlight. If there is simply not enough space, plant alpines in the crevices between paving slabs in a sunny part of the garden. Put them in the ground with some bone meal and leaf-mould packed around the roots, then spread a handful of coarse grit around the plants and under the leaves to stop them getting too sodden. Here are a few worth trying:

ALPINE CATCHFLY: Produces pink flowers on thick tufts of green leaves.

CAMPANULA COCHLEARIIFOLIA: A spreading perennial with clusters of pale blue, white, or pink bell-shaped flowers.

GENTIAN: A small blue evergreen perennial that is easily grown in rich soil.

IRISH MOLLY (*Viola x wittrockiana*): This tufted pansy flowers all season if deadheaded.

MAIDEN PINK: Producing white or pink flowers all summer, this perennial needs trimming after flowering.

MIMULUS: A deep-red beauty, the Chilean monkey musk arrived in Europe in 1838. Will flower from June to September and prefers less rich soil.

PRIMULA AURICULA: Produces yellow flowers from clumps of pale green leaves. An old-fashioned, drooping flower that is perfect for the edge of a raised bed.

PURPLE MOUNTAIN SAXIFRAGE: Preferring peaty soil and some shade, this saxifrage spreads quickly and produces large, cup-shaped flowers in spring. Other members of this plant family like the 'Dartington Double' (*Saxifraga moschata*) form clumps of dense leaves and loose-headed flowers.

SEA PINK (*Armeria maritima*): This hardy, clump-forming evergreen, also called 'thrift', has stiff stems producing many-flowered heads.

SEDUM: With cactus-like rosettes of fleshy leaves, sedum comes in many flowering and non-flowering varieties. *S. spurium* 'Schorbusser Blut' produces attractive red flowers, while 'Green Mantle' is good as ground cover.

Cacti and Succulents

As befits plants that come from the desert, cacti and succulents are usually kept indoors, and while they can cope with extreme heat and drought by storing moisture in their fleshy stems, roots or leaves, they are not hardy in a temperate climate. Most cacti have spines and all except the very large varieties will flower regularly. Cacti come in two distinct types: desert and rain forest. Of the first category, the *Mammillaria* is the largest genus of the cactus family and is mainly small and clump-forming. *Echinopsis*, the sea urchin cactus, produces beautiful flowers after three years, as does the closely related *Acanthocalycium* genus. *Opuntia* are strange plate-like cacti. All varieties must be kept in a warm atmosphere and need plenty of watering during the growth period. In winter, allow them to become dormant by putting them in a shaded spot and not watering them. Rainforest cacti, such as the *Schlumbergera* genus, need slightly different treatment and will benefit from being kept out of direct sunlight in summer. The compost should dry out between waterings.

Succulents are similar to cacti but without the spines and come mainly from South Africa. Popular examples include kalanchoe, seneccio 'Haworthii', crassula 'Morgan's Beauty' and the tree-like *Unicaria grandidieri* and *Euphorbia milothii*. All cacti and succulents are prone to fungal diseases and rot from overwatering. They will need re-potting at least every second year in a porous compost, with lots of sharp grit included in the mixture.

Five Favourite Perennials

- *Hellebore orientalis*
- *Geranium* 'Johnson's Blue'
- *Euphorbia characias wulfenii*
- *Osteospurnum ecklonis*
- Foxglove

10. Let's Go Veggie

Vegetables come from different parts of the plants we grow. Some are roots, such as carrots and parsnips, while others are fruits, like tomatoes and cucumber. We eat the leaves of cabbage and spinach and the stems of celery and rhubarb.

The idea of growing your own is appealing. Imagine being able to step outside your back door at any time and pick a fresh lettuce or a few spring onions, knowing exactly where they came from. That is the dream. The reality is that vegetable growing for the neophyte gardener is a challenge, especially since small tasty shoots are hugely attractive to slugs, mites, maggots, birds and other pests. One evening, you have a row of promising looking lettuce heads; next day all that is left are some chewed-up stalks. For even the most experienced of gardeners, this can be disappointing and frustrating.

Don't be put off – growing your own can be enormously rewarding. It is best to start small and gain confidence before becoming too ambitious. Ploughing up half the garden and putting down potatoes because everyone says that is the thing to do is not a good idea, unless you want to study the progress of potato blight at close quarters. An area of about 1m by 1.5m (6ft by 4ft) is quite adequate for the first year. If you find that your patch is a success, you can expand the following year.

Start with a plan, however basic. As the various vegetables take different nutrients from the soil, it is important not to plant crops in the same patch of ground every season, so if you want to stick with it, mark out a square of land where the crops can be rotated. This is the age-old system for avoiding disease, and divides vegetables into three categories: legumes (peas and beans); brassicas (the cabbage family) and everything else, including potatoes, onions, root and salad vegetables. This last category could be split into the onion family and potatoes, if you have the space.

Pick vegetables that are easy to grow, and sow sparingly until you get the hang of it. Starting off with cauliflower, however much you would like to examine how they grow, is foolhardy. An entire packet of cauliflower seeds went into my vegetable patch one year and not a single shoot appeared. Even potatoes, a staple in this part of the world, are not that easy. Carrots can fall victim to the carrot fly. Peas and beans need support. Vegetables such as aubergines and asparagus are not even to be contemplated until you have successfully grown at least a row of lettuce.

To make it even easier, establish which plants grow best in your part of the world. For example, in the temperate climate of north-west Europe, the blackberry bush grows wild and, if introduced to your garden, can turn it into a thicket within months. A reason to avoid it at all cost, some might argue. But who doesn't like blackberries? They are every bit as delicious as raspberries and strawberries and require virtually no effort because they are perfectly happy in the conditions that apply in north-west Europe. Grown as a hedge, they also provide a useful guard against intruders on a sunny back wall, thanks to their thorny stems. To keep them under control, all that is needed is regular pruning – and you'd do that for your roses, wouldn't you?

Likewise, there are sure to be plenty of vegetables that are native to your area and relatively easy to grow without requiring

24-hour-a-day attention. These include lettuce, scallions, French beans, broad beans, beetroot, parsnips, radish and leeks. For those with more exotic tastes, Swiss chard, rocket and mange tout grow easily, as does kohl rabi.

Preparation of the planned vegetable patch is vital. In November, dig over the patch you are going to use the following spring before the soil gets too cold. Remove stones and pebbles and add some well-rotted compost or fertilizer. In March, have another go at it. If the area you have picked is under grass, cover it with black plastic until the grass dies. This makes it easier to work.

Because young shoots are so vulnerable, even expert vegetable growers like to keep their germinating seeds indoors at first. Begin with a seedtray on a windowsill and when the plants are a few inches high, start hardening them off by putting them in a sheltered spot outside during the day, then covering them or bringing them back indoors at night. Alternatively, transplant them into your plot and protect them at night. Ideal for this purpose are empty 1.5 litre water bottles. Just cut off the bottom and then place over the shoot to make a miniature cloche. If you have a problem with birds, use special netting, available from your garden centre, to protect your growing crop. Plant in different parts of your garden; a small sheltered spot near my plum tree does not seem quite as attractive to the resident family of magpies as the other, more open space I had designated as my official 'vegetable patch'.

Label everything; you may think you will remember what you have done, but this is unlikely. Some seeds come with an identifying plastic label you can stick in the ground. If not, you can buy a packet of labels, remembering to write on them with a water-resistant pen. Alternatively, cut an old yoghurt carton into strips and use these as home-made labels. Since birds like to play with plastic, it is a good idea to draw a small sketch of your planting scheme as backup. What follows is a selective guide to growing a few common vegetables. Good luck!

BEETROOT: Not my own favourite vegetable, but since beetroot is easy to grow, it deserves inclusion here. The red globe varieties are the most common, although yellow and white varieties are also available and may be worth trying.

Beetroot seeds look like little bits of cork. Each of these contains several seeds. After soaking overnight to aid germination, they can be sown outdoors in April. If the soil is acid, apply lime to it in the previous autumn when preparing the seedbed. Place two seeds at a time in a shallow trench, leaving a 10cms (4ins) gap between each pair. Germination can take up to a fortnight. When thinning, throw out any poor specimens. After this, there should be no problems.

After harvesting, twist off the foliage rather than cut it, as this can cause 'bleeding'. If you choose to grow a yellow beetroot such as 'Burpee's Golden', the leaves can also be cooked.

BRUSSELS SPROUTS: One of the easier cabbage family members to grow, a Brussels sprout plant can shoot up to about 1m (3ft). One or two plants should give you all the Brussels sprouts you need over the winter. When the sprouts appear, pick them as you need them, starting at the bottom and working up. Sprouts need good quality, non-acid soil. For a winter crop, sow them in April indoors and plant out in June when the seedlings are about 15cms (6ins) high. Give them plenty of space, planting them about 60cms (2ft) apart. Protect from birds.

CARROTS: Be warned: carrots, highly popular though they are, are not easy to grow. In some parts, carrot fly is so endemic that it makes growing carrots a complete waste of time. Talk to your neighbours to find it is a problem where you live.

If you still want to try, first dig over the ground and remove large stones. Do not add fertilizer – any soil-enriching should be done the year before. Next check your soil, because carrots prefer slightly sandy conditions, which allow them to grow long, straight roots. Protecting the young plants will be your biggest task. To give the carrots a chance, sow thinly and away from tall plants. Cover with a fine mesh netting that will deter carrot fly.

Carrot

Taste in carrots continues to change. Increasingly popular are the new, smaller types that can be eaten raw. For the novice gardener, a medium-sized and proven variety, such as 'Chantenay Red Cored', or the fast-growing 'Nantes', is the safest bet. Seeds can be sown either under glass or cloches in March or unprotected in April. After that, the traditional method is to sow them with plenty of growing room so that thinning out will not be necessary. There is, however, another theory: that growing carrots closely together makes hoeing, which can damage the plants and attract carrot fly, unnecessary. Planting a row of onions near your carrots can also help keep off pests. If you survive all the hazards, your carrots should be ready to harvest between July and October.

LEEKS: There is not a lot that bothers a leek, making it another top choice for beginners. Leeks can withstand the bitterest of winters and are relatively immune to pests and diseases. From seed, they should be sown under glass in late January or February, or outdoors in April when the soil is warming up. Seedlings will appear in June when they can be thinned out. When they are about 20cms (8ins) high and as thick as a pencil, lift them gently with a kitchen fork and transplant into holes about 15cms (6ins) deep and filled with water. Leave about 15cms (6ins) between plants. To keep the stem white, build up the soil around the leek as it grows, being careful not to let it spill between the leaves. Alternatively, make tubes from newspaper and fill with potting compost, securing with rubber bands or string. Plant the seed in the compost. When the stems are half the thickness of a pencil, plant the entire tube into a hole in the ground.

LETTUCE: If most people were to grow just one vegetable, they would opt for lettuce. It seems so easy. Sadly it is not. As a plant, lettuce is susceptible to a depressing number of ailments, from mildew and grey mould to ring spot tipburn and mosaic virus. Lettuce grown under glass is even more susceptible to disease. The humble lettuce is a magnet for pests, including slugs and snails, aphids of one type of another, eelworms, cutworms and maggots. If your lettuce survives all that, it will not develop a heart if the soil is not rich enough, and even if it does, it can bolt, running to seed before it is ready for harvesting.

If you are prepared to tackle all these problems and watch your crop with an eagle eye, you can experiment with a huge number of varieties, few of which reach the supermarket shelves. Easiest to grow are the butterhead varieties, which spring up quickly, but are readily available and cheap to buy, so perhaps not worth the bother. Cos varieties grow upright and have crisp rather than soft leaves. Crisphead varieties include the popular iceberg with a tight heart and no loose outer leaves. Loose-leaf varieties do not produce a heart and include the decorative lollo rosa, with its distinctive red-tinged leaves.

To ensure a steady supply of lettuce all summer, sow a few seeds every fortnight. Sowing for the summer can begin under glass or indoors in early February, with planting out in March under cloches. Sowing outdoors can begin in March and continue until mid-July. This should give a steady supply of lettuce right into October. With cos varieties, leave the stumps of plants in the ground after the first picking to produce a second crop about six weeks later. Winter types can be sown in early August and will be ready for picking in November, while other varieties can be sown at the same time under cloches for cropping in spring.

Lettuce likes the sun and rich, well-drained soil, although it can be planted in any spare gap in the garden. If you have trouble getting lettuce seeds to germinate, put them in the fridge for a couple of days. When they are taken out again and sown, the seeds will 'think' winter is over and that it is time for them to sprout. Thin out your crop after the plants have grown to about 3cms (1ins) long. If you are losing the battle with the slugs, try planting your lettuce in a large pot, protecting the top with grease.

Pick your lettuce in the morning, when they are sweeter than later in the day. With non-hearting varieties, such as lollo rosa, simply pick the leaves you need from around the edges of the plant.

ONIONS: Onions are easy to grow. After preparing the ground with a suitable fertilizer, such as seaweed, you dig a trench, put in the seeds or, even better, the onions sets (the young plants which can be bought at the garden centre), cover them over and that's about it. Your onions are almost certain to flourish and so are a great confidence-builder. But whether or not they are worth growing is another story. Onions you grow yourself will not taste a great deal different from the ones you buy in the shop. However, there are plenty of unusual varieties to experiment with. Welsh onions have garlic-like bulbs on top of them. Japanese onions do not make a bulb at all but are ideal for salads and, since they are originally from the Orient, grow at a different time of the year to local varieties.

PEAS: There is nothing quite like the taste of a pea freshly picked from the garden, but peas are not easy to grow and unless you really have a passion for them, I wouldn't advise it. This is a vegetable that needs good quality, well-prepared, non-acid soil, a mild summer, and round-the-clock protection from birds.

Sowing time is late March when the soil has warmed up a bit, or perhaps a little later for marrow-fat varieties and mange-tout. Prepare a shallow trench about 5cms (2 ins) deep and press the seeds into the soil. Cover lightly and then protect with netting, using short stakes to keep this off the budding seeds. The seeds should germinate in about a week. When they reach about 8cms (3ins) in height, support them with canes. It is vital to keep the growing stems off the ground and away from slugs.

Peas do not like prolonged hot spells, so use a mulch to help keep the soil damp. After flowering begins, watch out for maggots. By about 12 weeks, the pods should be well filled and ready for picking. Start at the bottom of a stem and pick regularly.

POTATOES: Potatoes grow from sets, or seed potatoes, available in reputable garden centres. There is a huge variety to choose from, but the first choice is between 'earlies' and 'maincrop'. The first will provide 'new' potatoes early in the season; the second is a later crop. Early varieties may not provide the same volume of potato as a maincrop, but they are less likely to be hit by blight and are altogether an easier proposition.

Potatoes grow in almost any type of soil and are often used to help prepare a stretch of unused land before it is turned into a garden or vegetable plot. After harvesting, the land must be rested for two seasons before potatoes are grown in it again because of the risk of blight. But even if you are just growing potatoes to enrich your soil, prepare the land in the usual way before planting by digging it up the previous autumn and forking in plenty of well-rotted manure.

Seed potatoes should be bought in February and stored in trays; egg boxes are ideal for this purpose. After about six weeks they will sprout, a process known as 'chitting'. Now it is time to plant them. Dig a fairly wide trench, stick in your sets at a depth of about 15cms (5ins), keeping them at least 30cms (10ins) apart. Cover over and make a small ridge of earth. After the foliage, or 'haulm', starts to appear, cover this over as well – a process known as 'earthing up'. Water well and remove weeds when they appear. With 'earlies', the flowers open after about 13 weeks, which means they are ready for lifting. Dig down carefully to have a look and, if ready, remove carefully. With maincrop potatoes, planted from July until October, it will take a little longer, but one single set could provide up to 2kg (4lb) of potatoes. When harvesting, remove all traces of the potatoes from the soil to avoid disease in following years.

As for diseases, the most serious is the potato blight, cause of the Irish Famine in the mid-nineteenth century. Once blight takes hold, the entire crop will have to be destroyed. The first signs are brown patches on the leaves. Turn them over and you will see a white mould. Fortnightly spraying with a mixture of bluestone and washing soda is vital to prevent this happening. 'Earlies' avoid the problem as they are harvested before blight threatens. A number of other viruses can affect potatoes, while potato cyst, eelworm, slugs and wireworm can also cause problems. Fortunately, these are rare if good quality seeds are used and the crop is looked after carefully.

You can now grow potatoes in tubs; watch out for new varieties developed specifically for this purpose.

Radish

RADISHES: Radishes are simplicity itself to grow and the familiar red ones will be ready for eating about a month after sowing. Apart from the standard variety, often used as garnish, there are other types of radish well worth investigating. Planted in May for instance, mooli, or Japanese radish, produces edible roots up to 30cms (12ins) long.

Radishes will flourish in almost anything, but a well-prepared soil will ensure that they germinate and grow quickly. The seeds are best sown under cloches in January or February, or outdoors in March. Little or no thinning is required with summer varieties, unless the plants start crowding each other. Keep an eye out for weeds and water if the soil is dry, as all radishes need plenty of fluid to flourish and swell. The biggest problem is likely to be birds, who love the succulent young shoots.

RUNNER BEANS: With its red flowers, the runner bean is an attractive addition to the garden, climbing up bamboo stakes or along netting. It also produces a huge crop – up to 27kilos (60lb) for 3m (10ft) of plants – and is invaluable for increasing the nitrogen in the soil. But while runner beans may be popular, they require a lot of work. The soil must be well-prepared, and after sowing, careful watering is vital as the pods develop. In late summer, picking must be done every other day, even if you have to throw away some of your crop. Beans are susceptible to the usual hazards. In wet, cool years, mildew can occur, while the bean seed fly, the weevil and mice are among the pests that love beans.

Sow seeds only when all danger of frost has passed. Dig a couple of trenches about 1.5m (5ft) long and half a metre (18ins) apart. Place the seed in the trenches about 20cms (9ins) apart. The plants will need support as they grow. This can be done with a double line of inwardly sloping and crossed poles, steadied by a bar across the top. An alternative is to make a wigwam of three poles, placing a plant at the bottom of each.

Loosely tie young plants to the poles. Hoe regularly to keep weeds at bay and water regularly, occasionally using liquid feed during the cropping season. Above all, protect the plants from slugs and birds. Harvesting should continue for about eight weeks. Pick the beans regularly before they get to the 'stringy' stage, which means they might still appear small by commercial standards. If you have a glut, you can freeze your beans. To prepare, top and tail them and then blanch for two minutes. When they cool, place them in plastic bags or containers for the freezer. They will last for about a year.

Easier to grow are French beans, with several bush varieties available. Sow the seeds in May or June and the beans will be ready to pick just eight weeks later.

SHALLOTS: These small and strong-tasting onions grow in clusters and are extremely hardy. Plant the sets with about 15cms (6ins) between them before Christmas for harvesting in early summer.

SWISS CHARD: This tasty vegetable is included here largely because it is almost fool-proof to grow and is a good alternative to spinach. The only problem is likely to be slugs feasting on the young shoots, but that is a problem with all vegetables growing close to the ground.

Swiss chard

Swiss chard is part of the leaf beet family, which includes other easy-to-grow varieties such as spinach beet. When mature, it looks like a cross between celery and spinach, and has a pleasant flavour and crunchy consistency when cooked. To grow, sow your seeds outdoors in April and thin out to about 30cms (12ins) apart when the seedlings are large enough to handle. Keep weeds at bay and water if necessary. To harvest, pick off the outer leaves as they grow, being careful not to disturb the roots.

TOMATOES: Tomatoes are the roses of the vegetable world, attracting fanatical devotion from their followers. Some gardeners will grow no other vegetable and can describe the vagaries of every variety at length. Growing a tomato is supposed to be a complex and laborious activity, but I have managed to do it without any back-breaking effort and a good deal of enjoyment, so it cannot be that hard.

Tomatoes come in two basic varieties: the ones that grow upwards, known as cordon, and the ones that grow outwards, known as bush. Cordon varieties are easier to grow and are usually kept indoors or in a greenhouse. A sunny front porch is ideal. They should be encouraged to have one main stem that grows and fruits indefinitely and so any small shoots that appear must be removed immediately. One of the many plus points of attempting to grow your own tomatoes is that these shoots give off a wonderful aroma as you pull them off. If left to its own devices, such a tomato plant can grow close to a straggly 1.80m (6ft).

Growing tomatoes from seed is easy. You start in late February by sowing your seeds in a seed tray filled with compost, transplant them when the first leaves appear, and then move again into larger pots or grow-bags when they reach about 15cms (5ins) in height. At this stage, they will need support, so tie the main stem loosely to a well-fixed cane. Side-shoots are now your main concern as they can grow a couple of inches in a week. Remove as soon as you can get a proper hold on them. In early April, put down a few more seeds. To ensure an early crop, keep the plants in their small pots until the first flower truss has appeared and tiny fruits have formed. Planting out sooner can delay fruiting, as all the energy goes into growth rather than flowering.

To ensure a healthy crop, water carefully and feed with a special organic tomato fertilizer about once a week. Stop growth after the fourth truss has developed and remove any leaves below the first truss. Tap the supports occasionally to aid the growth of the fruit. You can pick your tomatoes either at the first sign of colour, ripening them off the vine, or wait until they are completely ripe, usually from August. Pick carefully, cutting the stem cleanly with a scissors or knife to reduce the chance of damaging the fruit. If you are a smoker, use gloves whenever you handle the plants, as tomatoes hate nicotine.

The biggest problem you will have growing tomatoes is picking a suitable variety. Many types of tomato have little or no flavour. Worth trying are 'Cherry Bell', a heavy cropper with an excellent flavour, 'Gardener's Delight', another heavy cropper, and 'Big Boy', a variety that produces huge fruits. Of the bush varieties, 'Alfresco' has a good resistance to disease, while 'Red Alert' has developed a solid reputation. Tomatoes grown outdoors generally have a better taste and if you choose a bush variety, you will not have quite as much work to do.

Germinate your seeds indoors and then transplant the seedlings to a sunny, sheltered spot where the soil has been well-prepared, and after all risk of frost has passed. Before planting, rake in a general fertilizer.

Cloches can help protect your young vegetables

 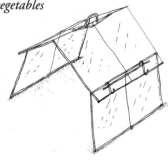

Top Tips for Tomatoes

   ◆ Don't sow too early – late February is fine

 ◆ Give each plant lots of room and plenty of light

       ◆ Use top quality compost or soil

 ◆ Follow the instructions strictly when using a feed

          ◆ Feed and water regularly

   ◆ Grow outside plants in full sun and against a
                white wall if possible

   ◆ Outdoors, grow in a different place each year
                      (rotate)

11. A Word on Herbs

Herbs can be defined as plants whose stems and leaves are used for flavouring food, though some herbs are grown for their scent or for medicinal purposes. For the novice gardener, herbs have much going for them. They look and smell good and, because they are relatively pest- and disease-free, they are easy to grow, especially if you buy them as small plants. Unlike flowers, herbs can be planted anywhere: in a small plot, between other plants in the garden, in pots or in window-boxes. All they ask is a little warmth and, with the minimum of attention, they will flourish.

As usual, before starting, it is worth formulating a plan. Ask yourself what kind of herbs you like and go for the ones you will use. If you are a fan of Indian cooking, coriander is a must. Mint can be an interesting addition to salads and smells lovely, basil is the perfect herb for Mediterranean-style cooking, while no kitchen should be without fresh parsley, chives and garlic. It is best and cheaper to grow herbs from seed, starting indoors from February. When the seedlings are strong enough to be lifted, pick them out carefully, using an ordinary kitchen fork, and place them in a larger pot for another couple of weeks' close attention before transferring them outdoors. New varieties of trailing herbs are available which would be perfect for a hanging basket just outside your kitchen door. Remember that all herbs like the sun and flourish in a light, well-drained soil.

BASIL: Not unsurprisingly for a herb associated with the Mediterranean, basil hates the cold and will not survive outdoors in winter. A half-hardy annual, it can be sown indoors from March, but should not be planted out until June and then only in a well-prepared seedbed getting plenty of sun. When they are large enough to handle, give the seedlings more space, leaving them about 30cms (1ft) apart. They can eventually grow to about 60cms (2ft) and produce small, white flowers. To avoid this, pinch out the top leaves when the plants are still small to ensure a good, bushy growth. The leaves are best when young; pick from June to September and, for drying purposes, before flowering starts. If you want your basil to survive the winter, remember to move it indoors as soon as there is a chill in the air.

BAY: The bay or laurel is an evergreen shrub or small tree that can grow to 3m (10ft) in height. In containers, when it reaches about 1m (3ft 4ins), it is snipped and sheared until it looks like a giant green lollipop. At this point, you can buy one, usually for an exorbitant price. Such a specimen is ideal for a porch or conservatory, where it will be protected from the damp and wind. For kitchen use, bay is best bought as a plant in the spring. So long as it is kept in a warm spot, it does not need too much attention, apart from plenty of watering in summer. Leaves are best picked while young and can be dried for winter use. A bay leaf, along with a sprig of parsley and of thyme, is an essential ingredient of a *bouquet garni*.

CHERVIL: Chervil, an annual, grows to about 45cms (18ins) and, unusually for a herb, is not too keen on direct sunlight. Its attractive fern-like leaves are used in soups and as an essential ingredient in omelette *fines herbes*. Sow from March in a shady spot, thinning out when strong enough to handle to give each plant enough space to grow.

Chives

CHIVES: Chives, that mild member of the onion family with its tubular leaves and purple flowers, has many uses and grows well in a sunny part of the garden. Because it can grow too easily, it should be planted in a special bag or small pot to help contain it. I have seen chives grow in a tarmacadam driveway. It can be sown from seed in March, but is less trouble to buy as a plant in the spring or autumn. Plant it in the ground, giving it about 20cms (8ins) of space and, every few years, pull it up gently and split it. Chives require regular watering. To use, cut off a number of stalks to within an inch of the soil. In May or June, get rid of any flowers before they open. Chives can be brought indoors for the winter, but if planted in a well-protected spot, will probably survive.

CORIANDER: Coriander looks a bit like parsley and, in both seed and leaf form, adds a distinctive flavour to food, and is typically associated with Indian cookery. The brown seeds resemble peppercorns and are not difficult to grow. Sow about 60cms (24ins) apart before covering them with a thin layer of soil. Firm this gently and keep moist and, in theory, you have a plant by August. It is easy to buy coriander in plant form, though this will also require careful handling and does not appreciate the cold. Harden it off by leaving it outdoors during the day and then in April, plant it in well-drained and well-

153

prepared soil. It should grow quite high, to about 45cms (18ins). Pick the leaves when you need them. To harvest the seeds, wait until the seed heads produce a pleasant spicy aroma at the end of summer. Collect the seeds and then spread them out to dry before storing them in closed jars or tins.

GARLIC: Garlic is easy to grow, or so say the experts. After all, the individual cloves sprout all on their own in the kitchen if they are left for a while. Unfortunately, when transferred to the ground, they may not flourish. This is all down to timing, as garlic needs about five weeks in a cold soil. Plant it in April by sticking the cloves of an ordinary head of garlic in the earth about 15cms (6ins) apart, with their tips (the narrow end) facing upwards just below the surface. There is nothing else to be done, apart from some watering if it gets too dry. When the leaves turn yellow in midsummer, lift the garlic with a fork, dry and store.

MARJORAM AND OREGANO: Sweet marjoram is a low bushy plant with white or purple flowers, growing to about 60cms (2ft). Oregano is a less-sweet variety of much the same plant. There is also pot marjoram, a perennial. Seeds should be sown annually indoors in March. In late May, plant the seedlings in a sunny spot, about 23cms (9ins) apart for sweet marjoram, and a bit more for pot marjoram. Both produce pale lilac flowers in the summer. Its grey-green leaves are often used as a substitute for thyme.

MINT: Mint is wonderful: great smell, lots of uses and not just with an Easter roast or on new potatoes. The problem with mint is its vigour, with its stems burrowing underground and then new plants popping up everywhere. So if you are planting straight into the soil, make sure your mint will be well restrained. There are special bags now available to help keep plants like mint from spreading, but an old bucket or a large flowerpot will do just as well. Anything smaller and you will find the mint bursting dramatically out of its container and suffocating any nearby plants.

To plant, dig a hole in the ground just large enough for the container and fill it to within 8cms (3ins) of the top with soil and compost. Put in your mint seeds and cover. In a few weeks, the mint will be ready for use. If planted like this, the mint will have to be re-potted and divided each spring. This is hard enough work, but still, better than having to uproot it all because it has become a nuisance. Mint comes in many varieties. Spearmint is the standard garden version, but there is also an apple mint, which has round leaves and a lovely aroma. Both red mint and pineapple mint have reddish leaves, while 'Bowles' mint' is good for mint sauce.

PARSLEY: The ever-popular parsley, rich in vitamin C and often used as a garnish, comes in a number of varieties, some curly, others flat. All flourish in rich, light soil and like shade, although the flat varieties are easier to grow. Parsley is a biennial, running to seed in its second season, and so should be sown around mid-March every year. Surprisingly, for a plant closely associated with temperate climates, germination is slow. To help germination, warm the seed drills by pouring hot water from a kettle into them. After sowing the seeds 25mm (1ins) deep and 30cms (12 ins) apart, expect to see nothing for at least a month. For big parsley fans, two sowings should be made, one in March or April for summer use and another in July for the winter. When it gets cold, the plants should be protected.

ROCKET: A few leaves of rocket can do wonders for a bland salad of iceberg lettuce. Although sold at 'luxury' prices in the supermarket, this is a plant that is stunningly easy to grow. Just get your seeds, throw them in the ground, cover lightly with soil, and wait a week or two. In my garden, rocket thrives anywhere – in the sun, in the shade, and between other shrubs and plants. The only problem can be greedy slugs. Pick the leaves off when you want them and, in the autumn, wait for the small pockets of seed to appear on the plant after flowering. When mature, pick these off your plant, let them dry and then scrape out the tiny seeds. Store these in a paper packet or glass jar and you need never again pay exorbitant prices for rocket leaves.

ROSEMARY: The flowers and stems, as well as the small, needle-like leaves of the evergreen rosemary shrub, can be used in cooking. This is a plant that likes a light, dry soil in a sunny, well-protected spot and will grow to about 2m (6ft) in height. It can be grown from seed or cuttings, or bought from any garden centre for planting in the spring. The bush will grow quite quickly, producing lilac-coloured flowers, and needs regular picking and pruning to keep it under control. It makes a dramatic border shrub.

SAGE: Sage is another evergreen shrub that loves the sun. Easily recognised by its highly aromatic and furry leaves, this is not an easy one to grow from seed, so buy a plant and place it outdoors in the spring. After it flowers, trim back a bit. The bushes, which can grow 60cms (2ft) high, become straggly and woody after three or four years and should be replaced.

TARRAGON: Tarragon is another herb that is difficult to grow from seed and best bought as a plant. It requires warm, dry soil and as it hates the cold, give it some protection in winter. As a plant that can grow almost 1.2m (4ft) tall and, like mint, spreads by a system of underground runners, tarragon needs controlling. Plant it outdoors in March, leaving it in a large pot to stop it spreading. Pick the leaves from June, before the green-white flowers appear.

THYME: Thyme is an evergreen and so, once planted, can

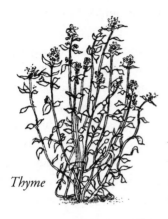

Thyme

be picked at any time of the year. Sow the seeds in spring and, after they germinate, thin them out to within 15cms (6ins) of each other. Thyme is another sun-lover, preferring a well-drained, sandy and warm spot in the garden. The plants should be divided every three years and replanted. Thyme is ideal for a windowsill pot. There are a number of varieties of thyme, with lemon thyme almost as ubiquitous as the common version. In summer, thyme flowers attract butterflies.

OTHERS: Angelica, balm, borage, camomile, caraway, dill, fennel, savory and sorrell are just some other herbs that can be grown. Lemon grass is one of the more unusual ones now available in seed form. Many herbs look as good as they smell, so take your pick!

HARVESTING YOUR HERBS: The best time to harvest herbs is in the early morning, after any dew or rain has dried off and before it gets too hot. At this point, the plant's oils are at their strongest. This is also the best time to water them. Stems and leaves should be picked when young and tender; flowers when they are in full bloom. Parsley, chives and chervil are best used fresh, though they can be frozen.

If not needed immediately, most herbs can be dried. Pick the leaves carefully to avoid bruising and then lay them on a flat tray, keeping the different herbs well separated. Leave in a warm, dry place, such as an airing cupboard, turning the leaves every day until they have dried out. After a week or two, put in a glass jar. If any moisture shows on the inside of the container, the herbs need more drying out. When they are definitely as dry as they are going to get, discard the stems and put the leaves, crumbled if necessary, in an airtight container. Store in a dark, cool place. Dry herbs with large leaves, such as bay, by tying them in bundles and hanging them in a cool, dry place.

Harvesting the seeds of herbs such as fennel, dill and coriander is simplicity itself. The seed pods which follow flowering are quite obvious even to a novice and should be picked when ripe, then placed indoors on trays and left to dry, when the seeds will be easy to remove.

Top Tips for Herbs

- Grow herbs anywhere in the garden.
- Put a pot or two of essentials, like parsley, on the kitchen window sill.
- Keep herbs well trimmed and lop off any flowers for a continuous supply of leaves.
- If you intend to bring your herbs indoors for the winter, keep them in easily portable containers.

---

12. Going to Pot

Travel, they say, broadens the mind and it has certainly had a huge influence on gardening practice. In the days of the 'Grand Tour', for instance, British noblemen and women returning home from Italy and France were full of plans to build orangeries on the scale they had witnessed on their visits. Back they would come with impressive collections of fine terracotta pots for their lemon and orange trees, forgetting that the climate in the British Isles is considerably chillier than in the rest of Europe. This led to the creation of elaborate greenhouses; but that is another story.

In continental Europe, where good soil is rare and cherished, keen gardeners concentrate on growing plants in tubs, window-boxes and hanging baskets. In summer, the smallest villages in Spain, France or the Alps are a riot of colour, thanks to the pelargoniums, jasmines and roses pouring out of tubs and windows. Unsurprisingly, this cheering practice has now spread everywhere you can find a garden centre. It means that the smallest of spaces can be turned into a miniature garden, while patios, porches and balconies can be transformed and walls brought to life. Even in a larger garden, pots and tubs can add colour and life to bare or neglected corners.

An interesting container becomes part of the display, and gardeners with an eye for the unusual are capable of using anything, from old watering cans to sinks, old chimney-pots and even wellington boots, as pots for their plants. For the more conventional, plastic containers and plain clay pots can be painted and dressed up.

When it comes to more delicate plants, growing them in a container that can be moved indoors when the weather turns cold will save the labour of planting out in spring and digging up again in autumn. Further good news is that many plants susceptible to slugs and other pests, or needing well-drained soil, will flourish in containers.

The soil in a tub is always warmer, which means plants grow faster. It is also easier to improve by adding compost or fertilizer. The only problem with putting plants in tubs is that you will need a kind neighbour to come in and water them if you are away for any length of time.

If you are going to put your tubs or containers in the garden, it is worth buying the biggest size you can find, as pots always seem to be smaller once you get them home. Anything can grow in a tub, so long as you prepare it properly. As in mainland Europe, pelargoniums will be a first choice for many, adding colour, flamboyance and perfume to the drabbest of surroundings right through to the autumn. Ideal for a window-box are the ivy-leafed varieties, which come mostly in shades of red, pink and mauve. Typically, these trail out over the top, but can also grow upright with the help of a few small twigs or stakes to prop them up. If you are looking for some yellow or orange as a contrast in colour, try the trailing gazania with its silvery leaves and bright daisy-like flowers.

Another favourite for container-growing is the fuchsia. Even the less hardy greenhouse-bred varieties will survive out of doors during the summer and have a flamboyance lacking in the more traditional varieties.

For permanent colour in the container, choose evergreen

shrubs such as box, yew, hebes or lavender, which often grow better when sheltered. Liven up your container with seasonal bedding plants such as hyacinth in winter, tulips in spring, and any one of a number of summer bedding plants once the weather gets warmer.

Simulate a border by putting pots in groups, as a single potted plant on its own can look a bit forlorn. The one exception might be at the front door, where a clipped bay or a conifer in an ornate pot or tub looks fine in isolation. Box can also be bought in pots and you can have fun clipping it into a ball or pyramid shape if that is your fancy.

A climber such as clematis can be made to wind around the doorframe from a judiciously placed pot if you cannot plant it in the ground. Put a clematis or honeysuckle in a large tub and train it up a trellis strong enough to take the strain after a few years of healthy growth. In the porch, arrange a collection of small pots around the base of one tall evergreen shrub to add colour. Use pots for growing tomatoes or even grapes.

Passers-by will enjoy hanging baskets or window-boxes, so try and make an eye-catching display, with a variety of plants of different heights. In a hanging basket, use tall plants in the centre and smaller, trailing ones around the edge. In a window-box, why not put a tall plant at one end, graduating to smaller plants and trailers at the other?

Patio Planting

Strictly speaking, a patio is an inner courtyard, but today the word has come to mean a hard or paved area used for eating out of doors. A patio will usually be at the back of the house and ideally, in a sunny, sheltered spot. It can be partially enclosed by trellis or fencing panels, or may include a pergola, all ideal for growing climbers. On a patio, containers come into their own. Place groups of pots and containers here, with a small tree perhaps to the back, a selection of colourful annuals to the front and some ferns or ivies as foliage. Some houseplants can also be brought outdoors for the summer.

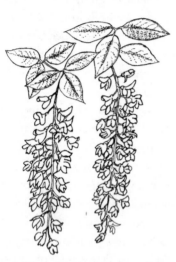

The yellow tassels of the laburnum

Groups of pots can be used to add interest to a lawn and will look even better if placed on a bed of gravel or pebbles that will make them stand out against the green of the grass.

Plants with large leaves, such as the **yucca** or **phormium**, and small shrubs like the **Japanese maple** or **acer**, can be used for dramatic effect if grown in a nice tub. When they grow too big, plant them out. Other trees that grow well in containers include **laburnums**, **dwarf apple trees**, small **willows** and the **ornamental pear** or **flowering cherry**. These will need a pot at least 38cms (15ins) deep and proportionately wide, but don't worry: they will not grow too big for their container because the restricted space will have a bonsai-like effect on their expanding roots.

Shrubs that are happy in containers include **camellias**, **rhododendrons** and **azaleas**, as well as most **herbs**. **Hebes** can make good container plants, as can some varieties of **viburnum**, such as *viburnum tinus*, with its little clumps of black berries in winter. Few gardeners bother putting border perennials into containers, but these can also work well. Try any of the many **ornamental grasses** and **ferns** for a start.

On a balcony, plants can be grown in lightweight containers or in growing-bags and it may be possible to put a trellis on one side, giving support for climbers. Ideally, put most plants towards the front of the balcony where the light is better. Plants that do not mind shade, such as some forms of **fuchsia**, **begonia** and **polyanthus**, can be arranged at the back. Window-boxes, with a selection of colourful annuals and trailing plants to spill out over the sides, can be hung securely over the top of the balcony walls. There are even mini-greenhouses that can be put on balconies to be used for growing new plants and sheltering existing ones over the winter.

The ideal window-box is made of wood with a minimum depth and width of 25cms (10ins). With a wide window, it may be better to have two boxes. Expensive clay boxes are also available but could be too heavy for the average windowsill. To ensure good drainage, the window-box should be raised slightly above the sill, using small wedges of wood if necessary. Fix it firmly to the wall with strong brackets.

When it comes to the pots themselves, the choice is between plastic and clay. Plastic pots are cheap and cheerful, and because they are so light, are easy to move. But they are not great for plants that like well-drained soil, and can become brittle with age.

Clay pots are more attractive, but because they are porous, the soil inside can dry out quickly and they will leave an ugly tide-mark wherever they are left standing – worth considering if you are putting a few on a wooden windowsill. They are perfect for plants needing well-drained soil and, because they are heavy, ideal for large plants. On the minus side, they are easily broken and impossible to clean. Here's a tip to get that new, orange look off clay pots: attract algae and moss by painting them with a mixture of manure water (soak some manure in a bucket and then drain off the water), milk and liquid fertilizer.

The larger urns and jars come in literally any shape or style, many aping the designs of the Greeks and Romans a couple of millennia ago. Tubs are large, deep containers that can be used for permanent plants, such as shrubs, trees and climbers. A wooden container is still the best for this purpose and a variety of half-barrel or square designs can be bought from garden centres. Stand these on blocks of wood or stone to ensure good drainage. Full-sized barrels can also be used, but are most often seen with planting holes in their sides, usually for strawberries. The barrel is filled with compost and the roots of the strawberries are pushed through the holes, with a couple more going on top. Barrels can also be used for alpines and for bedding plants like lobelias and petunias. Troughs can be put on the ground under a window. Coming in a variety of materials, with the old stone varieties particularly prized, these must be placed on brick or blocks of wood to guarantee good drainage.

Planters are very large containers used for groups of plants rather than one single specimen and giving better scope for imaginative colour schemes. Like tubs, planters should be raised off the ground.

There are different views on what soil to use in containers. Most argue that a heavy potting soil is needed to help weigh the pot down and stop it falling over in windy conditions, but others feel that the lighter the soil the better, so that the pot can be moved easily. Bags of compost specially formulated for containers are widely available.

To prepare a tub or container, place bits of broken clay pots, stones, broken up polystyrene or broken up twigs over the hole at the bottom to ensure good drainage. Next, part-fill with a heavy, loam-based potting soil to give the pot stability. After soaking the plant well, remove it from its container and carefully tease out knotted roots. Put it in the tub and test for position and size, adding and taking away soil as needed. Firm the compost around the roots. The soil level should be about 2.5-5cms (1-2ins) below the rim of the pot, to allow for watering.

The traditional hanging basket is made from galvanised wire hanging from a chain, although solid plastic versions are now available. To prepare, first fill with sphagnum moss and a liner made from one of several materials, most usually felt, foam or recycled wool. Use old newspapers or knitwear for a home-made liner. Alternatively, plastic sheeting with drainage holes is also available. Next fill with compost and, if you like, push trailing plants through the wires, roots first, as the container is being filled. Wrap the plants in small pieces of polythene shaped into narrow cones so they will not get damaged as they are pulled through. Then use a sharp knife to cut a hole in the lining and work the plant through carefully, removing the polythene when you are finished. Do all this in the shade if possible. Leave a watering space on top of about 2.5cms (1in). If you wish, an old saucer or aluminium pie dish can be placed in the container under the moss to act as a water reservoir.

Solid baskets are simply filled with compost and plants arranged on top, with upright plants in the middle and trailers to the sides. Baskets are difficult enough to maintain and need regular watering, especially in summer when they dry out quickly. Once plants are coming into flower, feeding is a must, as the regular watering tends to leech the goodness from the original compost. If the compost becomes so dry that the water is running off the top of it, add a few drops of washing-up liquid to the water. If even this is not enough, take down the basket, lower it into a basin of water and leave until the compost looks moist again. Then stand in the shade until the plants revive.

The ritual of watering and feeding can be a problem with hanging baskets. Put them too low and you bump into them; place them too high and you need a step-ladder to get at them. The best option is the pulley system now widely available in garden centres or hardware stores.

What to Plant

There are a number of attractive plant combinations that can be used in tubs and boxes over the summer. Here are a few suggestions:

- A combination of bush and trailing fuchsias with a begonia *semperflorens.*
- Zonal and ivy-leaved pelargoniums with ageratum and begonias.
- Tree mallows and zonal pelargoniums, with silver-leafed cineraria and chlorophytum.
- Climbing black-eyed Susan (*thunbergia alata*) with trailing nasturtiums.
- Morning glory or climbing ipomoea, French marigolds and trailing petunias.

In spring, go for an assortment of bulbs, while in winter, used winter-flowering pansies. Good annuals for containers include verbena, viola, begonia, schizanthus, petunia, nemesia *strumosa*, swan river daisy, wallflower, lobelia, and Busy Lizzie.

Most of these are perennials grown as annuals or half-hardy annuals; in other words, they have to be uprooted each year.

Watering

In winter at least, container plants do not need to be watered daily; too-frequent watering can rot the roots and kill the plant. Before watering, have a good look at the compost; thoroughly soaked compost will have a healthy, dark colour, while dried-out compost will be lighter. To test whether your container or pot plants need watering, push your finger into the compost. If it feels dry, then it is safe to water. When it is still damp, leave well enough alone. Weight is another guide, as a well-watered pot will feel distinctly heavier than a parched one. If you do not trust your own judgement, buy a small 'moisture meter' kit that will tell you how much moisture is left in the soil.

When you make the decision to water, be generous and pour on enough to soak the compost right through. The rate of drying out will depend on the weather and the time of year. During a hot, dry spell, it is not unknown for container plants to need watering twice a day, while in winter, once a week may well suffice and indeed, some plants need no watering at all.

The water in your tap is likely to be either hard, with lots of lime, or soft, with little or no lime; if there is a constant crust of limescale in your kettle, or orange-coloured stains in the sink or bath, you know that your water is hard. Lime-hating plants, such as rhododendrons and camellias, will not like hard water. The solution is to use rainwater collected outside in a butt or barrel. It is always best to use water that is at the same temperature as the atmosphere. For indoor plants, this means that the water should be lukewarm.

Feeding

A hungry plant will quickly leech the soil of nutrients and this is especially true of container plants. All plants need the Big Three – nitrogen, phosphorus and potash – if they are to thrive. Fertilizers are applied only in the growing period; do not ever feed in winter as your plants are dormant during this period and any fertilizer applied could build up and rot the roots. From early spring, feed about once a fortnight, or once a week if the plant completely fills its container. Fertilizers for containers are available in slow-release tablet or spike form; just push these into the compost and forget about them for a month or so.

The better-known brands of fertilizer will be sold either as granules that can be sprinkled on the soil's surface or as a liquid that should be diluted with water and then sprinkled or poured on. For flowering and fruiting plants, such as tomatoes, you can buy a special potash-rich organic fertilizer, but otherwise, go for the standard types containing about 7 per cent of the three main nutrients plus some trace elements.

You may occasionally need to use a fertilizer with just one of the elements. Sulphate of ammonia supplies nitrogen and will help the stems and leaves grow, super-phosphate is rich in the phosphorous needed by the developing roots of seedlings and young plants, while sulphate of potash helps boost flowering and fruiting. Organic versions are readily available.

If your plant is wilting for no good reason, a quick boost with a special liquid fertilizer, sprayed directly on to the leaves, may help to revive them. This type of foliar feed is for emergencies only and must not be used as a substitute for standard feeding.

Compost will also need to be replaced about every two

years. As an alternative to re-potting, especially in large containers, remove the top 2.5cms (1ins) of compost in spring and replace it.

Repotting and Potting On

Plants cannot remain in the same container forever. If they are becoming pot-bound, they will need to be moved into bigger containers and, even if they still look healthy, the compost in their container should be replaced. To check the plant's roots, tap the plant carefully out of the pot and have a look. If the compost is a mass of roots, it is time for a larger container. Pick one no more than two sizes up, as plants will not become established if there is too much compost around their roots. Prepare the new pot in the usual way, placing broken clay pots over the drainage holes and protecting these with some twigs and leaf-mould before putting in the compost.

To replace the compost in a big container, a second pair of hands is needed. First lay the container on its side. One person then holds the pot, tapping it gently around the rim with a piece of wood, while the other gently pulls out the plant. When the plant is free, examine the root-ball, teasing away the surrounding compost. Before replacing the compost, the container must be thoroughly washed and dried. Put some compost in the bottom of the pot, replace the plant and fill the pot to the top. Before firming down the surface, move the plant gently around in the pot to get the new compost worked in between its roots. Water well.

Five Good Plants for Containers

- Strawberry tree (*Arbutus unedo*)
  - Miniature apple tree
  - Japanese maple
  - Bay (*Laurel nobilis*)
  - Box

13. Putting It All Together

There are two main styles of garden. In the formal style, going back to the time of Louis XIV in France, you will find straight lines, flowerbeds in geometric squares and circles, and tight hedging, usually of yew or box. This style flourished at a time when those wealthy enough to own a garden could call on a fleet of lackeys to do the hard work. Today, the formal style continues in public parks, where stunning displays of neatly arranged annuals can appear in flowerbeds overnight. The informal style, with gentler lines and flowers spilling out of herbaceous borders, emerged in Victorian times. While it certainly looks a lot more relaxed, a lot of work goes into producing the perfect border.

Most of us will take a bit from both styles for the rectangular piece of land to the back of our typical suburban house. The herbaceous border may seem like too much work, so we shall go for a mixed border, based on easy-to-maintain shrubs and perennials, with some bedding thrown in for colour. Curved lines may not suit our space, so we opt for straight paths and square shapes – and nothing wrong with that. Like all gardeners before us, we shall find a style that suits our needs.

In a new house, you may be starting completely fresh; in an older one, you will certainly have an established garden and someone else's ideas to deal with. So first decide what you need from your garden, especially at the back of your house. If you have children, a hardwearing stretch of grass is probably a good idea. If children aren't an issue, you can have a freer hand when it comes to planting, since over-exhuberant play will not be a problem. If you have pets, you will quickly find that they have their own plans for the garden. Even a medium-sized dog can soon wear down a path to his favourite spot, so it might be worth putting down a path where one is going to appear anyway.

Most people will start their garden in a haphazard manner, sticking in a few shrubs, maybe planting a favourite tree, but not really knowing what they want to do. Over the years, they may change the shape of a path or a lawn, add a patio, put in decking and move the original plants around. The serious gardening books tell you that time and money can be saved if you know what you want from the start and you concentrate on one part of the garden at a time. But surely this takes away from the fun that creating a garden over a number of years is all about? Mixing and matching, discovering various plants and flowers, seeing how they behave and then finding them a place that suits them is a slow but infinitely rewarding experience. One year, you may be obsessed with poppies; the next year, it could be delphiniums. Learning about plants will take years, but with so many thousands to choose from, it is an absorbing and completely personal experience.

In my own north-facing back garden, I cleared out the old bramble-infested jungle in the back yard and, knowing nothing at the time, got a gardener friend to plant a line of shrubs in a 1m (3ft) wide border at the back. The trouble with this border is that an ancient cedar from next door overshadows it completely, parching the soil and making it a considerable challenge that I haven't got to grips with even yet. Back then, I could just about tell the difference between a fuchsia and a rose. When my friend asked me what shrubs I wanted, I could not answer him.

Shrubs – what were they? So he picked a few of his own favourites, told me to watch how they grew for a few seasons, see which ones I liked and then move them around. He picked well – among the mature shrubs I now have gracing my garden are some gorgeous, delicate hebes, photinia 'Red Robin', a Mexican orange flower, a rock rose, some fuchsia, a creeping cotoneaster, a few viburnums and senecios and a cherry laurel, with delicate spikes of white flowers. I love them all !

I took longer to make up my mind about the front garden, after removing the appalling griselinia, the conifers and an overgrown heather. Already taking advantage of its south-facing aspect and rich soil are a magnolia, a Japanese acer and a small willow, along with a collection of maturing shrubs and perennials. Parts of it I like, while the rest changes from year to year, as my tastes evolve. Get in the professionals, you say, but I don't know about that. They would probably propose cutting back the lawn, putting in some trendy bricking, then digging up what is left and planting a completely predictable collection of shrubs. They might possibly suggest that keeping the griselinia would have been a good thing, since most of them clearly love this ghastly plant. You don't believe me? Just wander around and take a good look at any garden that has been refurbished by professionals.

I have nothing against professional gardeners, but it is amazing how easy it is to pick out their handiwork when they hit on a client who gives them a free hand. So even if you plan on getting someone in, do some research first; gardeners tend to stick to their own favourite and pretty limited collection of plants, so be ready with some ideas of your own. That way, you will not find yourself with a yawn-inducing collection of plants that you can see in every other garden nearby. A garden is for life, not just for next year.

So here is a summary of what I now believe: if the garden is already well planted, have a good look at everything, do a bit of clipping and cutting back and then think hard. Get the advice of a gardener, or even better, a friend who gardens. You may discover that you have some really nice specimens that would be expensive and slow to replace. Years of love and attention will have gone into a well-stocked garden, so treat it with respect, even if it is not your style. After a tidy-up, leave everything and see how it all develops over a year or so.

If the garden has turned into a thicket, you will have no alternative but to hack your way through it and remove everything. With a bit of luck, it will be autumn and you can then do some hard digging on borders and flowerbeds, leaving the winter frost to break up the clods. Mix in some top-quality manure or compost while you are at it, using about a bucket-ful per square metre. A priority should be to choose a spot for your compost heap and maybe a garden shed. After that, put down a few bulbs, but otherwise wait until the spring and buy in a collection of annuals, including climbers like sweet pea and nasturtium varieties that can be trailed up bamboo pools or trellis to give you a temporary screen. After living with this for the summer, you will have a much better idea of what appeals to you in colours and shapes.

Whatever you may think from watching television gardening make-over programmes, it is the plants that will transform your garden, not a startling piece of sculpture, and if you want a new look, the easiest and cheapest way to get it is by sowing and planting. For this, you may need help, but why not go for it yourself? You may not get it right at first, but you will learn a lot and have the satisfaction of creating something that is entirely yours.

To get some ideas, walk around your neighbourhood and

take a good look at what is growing in already established gardens. You will find that few are very elaborate and that most are based around a surprisingly small number of plants. You will learn what grows easily in your area and probably discover a few absolute gems of gardens, lovingly put together by their owners, and a true inspiration. Next, head for a couple of garden centres and examine their stock, taking plenty of time. Most will specialise in particular plants that they either grow themselves or import. So while one centre will have dozens of hebes or clematis, another may concentrate on a huge choice of heathers. Take note of the prices because these can vary enormously. If you want a tree, you can assume that the bigger they are, the more expensive they will be; there are companies doing very well out of supplying 'instant trees', mostly to commercial institutions. But even in an ordinary garden centre, you will find 1m (3ft) high black bamboos, trimmed laurel bushes, shoulder-high Japanese maples and magnolias, all at very fancy prices. You may be tempted, but buy these young and they will cost little more than a standard rose or clematis. They are also likely to settle much better in your garden and will grow faster than you expect.

If you are starting a new garden, the first big decision is where to put what the professionals call the 'the hard landscaping', such as paths, patios and maybe a small terrace for a barbeque. The paths should give you easy access to the parts of the garden you use most and there are lots of new materials to experiment with at the moment. Bricks can be laid in a variety of patterns and even the much-maligned concrete slabs can look quite well when softened by strips of pebble or gravel or by bricks placed between the slabs. Where the lawn edges on to the flowerbeds, it may be worth putting in a 'mowing edge' with paving stones that the wheels of the lawnmower can run along. Railway sleepers have many uses and can be used as paths or an alternative to decking.

Ideally, the area outside the back of your house will form a natural patio. But if the back is north-facing, you will probably find that the warmest spot in the garden is at the end and then you have the problem of creating a sheltered paved area not overlooked by neighbouring windows.

Ask yourself if you really need a conventional hedge. Many suburban front gardens are ruined by the overuse of heavy, evergreen hedging in an attempt to give the house 'privacy'. Unless your house is situated well away from the road, this is a fruitless task. A mixture of a few nice shrubs and small trees might be a better option. As for the back garden, a trellis fixed to the wall, with a climber, such as a clematis, honeysuckle or rose, trailed through it, could prove a more flexible alternative to hedging and will take up far less space. A well-placed garden shed can also help create a sense of privacy, while there are all sorts of interesting screens, arches and garden dividers now for sale. Use your imagination!

If you want a border hedge, box is particularly good for low hedging, while hawthorn, escallonia and beech, alone or mixed, are other choices.

When it comes to the flowerbeds, think big. Whatever you grow will certainly turn out to be larger than you expected. The ideal border should be at least 3m (10ft) in depth to allow for a good mixture of plants, and however large it is, you will wish it were even bigger.

Next decision is where to put your trees, smaller hedges and shrubs; the 'living structure' of the garden. It is important to get a good balance between deciduous and evergreen. Too much evergreen and the garden will seem very dull in the warmer months; too little and winter will be horribly bleak.

Small trees and shrubs fall into two categories: those that should be given plenty of space to develop, such as a magnolia, acer or crab apple, and others that will fit into the mixed border. These would include weigela, broom (*Genista*), blue beard (*Caryopteris*), Cape fuchsia (*Phygelius*), mock orange (*Philadelphus*), smoke tree (*Cotinus coggygria*) and various types of hebe, as well as the ubiquitous hydrangea and buddleia.

Every well-designed garden needs a focal point. This could be a dramatic tree or plant or even the garden shed, placed with a bit of thought and decorated with a climber trained around it. Pergolas, a well-placed bench, an archway, or a raised terrace are other ideas that need not be too expensive and do not take up valuable planting space. Water features have also become very popular.

When it comes to the borders, a mixed border should command the sunniest spot in the garden. Rockeries or a raised bed also need plenty of sun and so may not be suitable for every garden. For the perfect mixed border, you must know how each plant you put in is going to behave. You should have a colour scheme in mind. Some people love pinks and purples, while others prefer yellows and creams. A mixture of these two could look horrible, particularly if you put in some bright red as well. As for the plants themselves, those from much the same natural habitat look better together. It is also worth knowing whether or not your plant objects to being moved around. If you are undecided about what you are doing, go for plants like ground-covering geraniums, campanula and phlox which can be uprooted and replanted without lasting damage.

There are five distinct plant shapes to consider when designing a garden:

1. Spiky plants, like grasses or, in larger form, the yucca or

phormium, with their spear-like leaves, are eye-catching and need careful placing.

2. Large, flat plants such as hosta, with their fleshy foliage, stay low and are best planted in groups on the edge of a border.

3. Ferns, with their lacy leaves, can lighten the effect of an over-leafy bed.

4. The rounded hummock-style plants, such as lavender, small hebe, sage and artemesia, add a softer, gentler note.

5. Finally, vertical plants, like the yew or the juniper, grow upwards and straight and can be clipped for dramatic effect.

Co-ordinating it all is a matter of taste. Repeating the same plant at intervals will tidy up a bed that is getting out of control. Contrasting swathes of low-lying specimens, such as geraniums, with something upright and spiky, like a grass, is another trick. To add drama to a bland flowerbed, use big, bold plants such as a yucca, a Scotch thistle, or a giant fennel.

If you don't have much space, put all the bright, extrovert colours into one 'hot' bed and the cooler hues in another. Designers argue that it is best to put colour schemes with red, orange or bright yellow near the house and the cooler shades farther away to create a sense of distance, especially in the evening, but this may not always be possible, particularly in a north-facing garden. Lighter-coloured and variegated plants, such as winter jasmine and euonymous, will cheer up a shaded area near the house.

As for other colour schemes, in a border with a variety of red plants, such as fuchsia, dahlia, penstemon, lobelia, poppy and verbena, add some coolness with *rosa glauca*, a berberis such as *b. thunbergeii* or even a dwarf-leafed phormium. For a gentler border, mix yellows, greys and soft purples. Don't forget that some vegetables can fit very well into a flowerbed; runner beans were originally planted for their small flowers rather than for their edible pods and twine beautifully around an archway with a few sweets peas.

You will find that you develop certain passions and interests after a few years of experimentation. There is no harm in specialising – most of the classic plants have enough variety within their species to feed a life-long obsession. Orchids, peonies, tulips, roses and even dahlias all have devoted fans who barely look at any other species. Whatever you fancy, it will quickly become clear that some plants will flourish in your garden, while others die. Trying to change your soil long-term will not work, so it is up to you to find out which plants grow well and which don't. You will also get to know the good and bad corners of your garden and find that a plant that struggles on one side will love the other, or that the conditions out front favour very different plants from those at the back.

It's all before you – and it does not even need much work. An hour or two each week watering, weeding and tidying, will not only keep most gardens in order but will provide you with something unique and special that is completely your own. Go for it!

APPENDICES

A Word about Latin

Firstly let's deal with those Latin names. The translation of rose into 'rosa' is simple enough, while the generic word 'narcissus' is used for the entire daffodil family, and words such as crocus and forsythia are Latin anyway. But how about *ilex* for holly, *galanthus* for snowdrop and *dianthus* for sweet william?

The good news is that wherever you go in the world, you will find that plants are called by those same Latin names; it has become the universal language of the garden. Plants are looked at first for their organs of reproduction, then for their leaves and finally for their flowers. The naming of a plant begins with its genus. This is the name of a group of plants that are physically similar, such as rosa or pelargonium. A genus consists of a number of species, this being defined as a group of plants that can cross-fertilize one another. So the common bedding geranium group is called *Pelargonium hortorum*. This in turn is divided into many variations of flower, size and colour, not all of them clear-cut. So after your genus name, often contracted to a single letter, 'P' for instance in the case of geraniums, and its species, comes another group of words, often in English, such as 'Red Elite' or 'Multibloom Mixed' or 'Mrs Henry Cox'. Cultivated varieties like these often get fancy names and are officially called 'cultivars', since they don't come from nature like true varieties.

Certain words need little explanation. '*Compactum*', for instance, would be a dwarf plant, while '*hybrida*' clearly means hybrid. When names are preceded by an 'x', this means a cross between two different species. The Michaelmas daisy, *Aster x frikartii*, for instance, is a hybrid of *Aster amellus* and *Aster thomsonii*.

Other words will tell you even more about the plant. '*Albus*' means white, '*nana*' dwarf, '*repens*' creeping, '*odoratus*' scented, '*vulgaris*' common and '*aestivalis*' summer-flowering. You could end up learning to love your Latin.

Glossary

ACID : Soil with a pH value of less than 7; lacking in lime and preferred by heathers, rhododendrons, camellias and potatoes. Most garden plants prefer a slightly acid soil (about 6.5pH).

AERATING: Compacted soil in the lawn or borders will need aerating to help drainage and promote growth. Use a fork to pierce 15cms (6ins) holes in the ground at regular 8cms (3ins) intervals. If you have problems with moss, use a hollow-tined fork. For big jobs, hire an aerating machine.

ALKALINE: Soil with a pH value of over 7; lime-rich. Preferred by carnations, cabbage, viburnum, rock roses and wallflowers, but few other plants. In limestone areas, the tap water is often strongly alkaline or 'hard' and may be bad for pot plants.

ANNUALS: Plants that are sown, flower and die in a single year.

ANTHER: The part of the stamen that produces pollen.

BIENNIALS: A plant with a two-year cycle, growing from seed into a small plant in the first year, then flowering, producing seed and dying in the next.

BULB: True bulbs are like plants in waiting – peel away the outside layer of dried leaf and inside you'll find new leaves waiting for a chance to display themselves. The bulb of an onion or tulip consists of a flattened stem bearing a central shoot surrounded by those fleshy inner leaves with thin brown ones on the outside. Compare corm and rhizome.

CACTUS: Cacti, belonging to a larger group called succulents, have a swollen stem, protected by prickly spines that in their desert habitat, allows them to survive in periods of drought. They like heat, don't need much watering and are easy to grow from seed.

CALYX: The outer 'skirt' of a flower, usually small and green, but sometimes showy and brightly coloured. It is formed from the sepals and encloses the petals in a bud.

CATKINS: The furry shoots or flowers produced by woody shrubs and trees such as the willow, hazel, birch and alder.

CLOCHE: Bell-shaped cover in glass or plastic which can be placed over a plant to protect it from birds, pests and the cold.

COLD FRAME: An unheated wooden or concrete frame with a glass top, used to protect young plants and seedlings outdoors.

COMPOST: Mixture of decomposed vegetable matter or manure used as fertilizer.

CONIFER: A shrub or tree that produces cones and is usually but not always evergreen, with narrow, needle-like leaves.

CORM: These look like slightly flattened bulbs, with a globular stem base surrounded by papery scale leaves. As the growing plant uses up the food stored in its corm, this shrivels up and smaller corms grow on top of the old one. Crocus and gladioli are corms.

COROLLA: The part of a flower formed by the petals.

CULTIVAR: A contraction of 'cultivated variety'. A variety of plant that was produced from a natural species and is maintained by cultivation.

CUTTING: The pieces of a plant that are cut or pulled off a parent plant, then planted so that they can produce roots of their own. Shoots, stems, leaves and roots can all be used as cuttings.

DEADHEADING: The removal of fading flower heads from a plant to encourage more growth. With long-stemmed plants, cut each stem back to the next growth point or set of leaves.

DECIDUOUS: In plants the loss of leaves at the end of the growing season.

DIVISION: Dividing a plant clump into several parts during its dormant period for propagation purposes.

DORMANCY: The period when growing stops or slows down. Ideally, shrubs and small trees should be planted or moved during this period.

ESPALIER TREES: Trees, usually apple or pear, with branches fixed to horizontal supports on walls.

EVERGREEN: Retaining its colour all year round, with old leaves shed a few at a time, rather than all together, as in deciduous plants. In cold climates, semi-evergreens lose older leaves after new ones are produced.

F1 HYBRIDS: Refers to the first generation of plants produced by crossing two other plants. These tend to be more uniform and vigorous. If you plant their seeds, you will produce F2 plants, usually not as vigorous as their parent plant.

FLORET: A single flower in a head of many flowers.

FLOWER: The part of the plant containing the reproductive organs, surrounded by sepals and petals.

FLOWER HEAD: A mass of small flowers or florets that together appear to form a single flower.

FRIABLE: Crumbly and easy to work; used to describe good soil.

GENUS: A category in plant classification, consisting of a group of related species.

GRAFTING: Method of propagation by artificially putting two different plants together to form a single new plant. One plant is used for the roots; the other for the shoots and the two then bound together until they grow into one. This system is often used for plants, such as modern roses, that do not grow well from cuttings.

HALF-HARDY: Plants that need protection when frost or cold winds are expected. Will withstand temperatures down to about 0°C (32°F). *Half-hardy annuals*: Sow under glass in spring or outside in early summer. *Half-hardy perennials*: Plant out in summer; bring inside during the winter.

HARDY: Plants that can live out of doors all year, even through the winter, and are capable of withstanding temperatures as low as -15°C (5°F). There are also borderline hardy trees and shrubs that need mild winters to flourish. *Hardy annual*: Sow outside in spring for summer flowering. *Hardy biennials*: Sow outside in early summer for flowering the following year. *Hardy perennials*: Plant permanently outside in a bed or border.

HERBACEOUS PERENNIALS: A group of plants with non-woody stems which die down every winter. New growth appears from underground in spring. These plants form clumps which grow and spread over the years. Control this by digging up and dividing every few years.

HUMUS: The organic residue of decayed vegetable matter in soil. Often used to describe partly decayed matter, such as leaf-mould or compost.

HYBRID: The offspring of genetically different parents, usually produced by artificial cultivation, but occasionally occurring in the wild.

LIME: Compounds of calcium; the amount of lime in a soil determines whether it is acid, alkaline or neutral. Most plants like a little lime.

LOAM: Good soil, combining the best attributes of clay, sand and silt.

MANURE: Animal excreta, usually with straw added, used to fertilize soil.

MULCH: A layer of material applied to the soil, usually around a plant to conserve moisture, protect the roots from frost, discourage weeds and enrich the soil. Can come as rotted manure, garden compost, chipped bark, black polythene or gravel.

NEUTRAL: When soil has a pH value of 7, making it neither acid nor alkaline.

PERENNIALS: Plants that live for at least three seasons.

PETIOLE: The stalk of a leaf.

PINCH OUT: The removal by hand of the top set of young leaves from a plant to encourage more growth and a better size.

PROPAGATOR: A structure that provides a protected and humid atmosphere for seedlings and cuttings.

RHIZOME: Creeping stems that grow just under the soil surface, sending up leafy shoots, wherever there is a bud. The iris and bamboo produce rhizomes, but unfortunately so do a number of rampant weeds. When removing these, make sure to pull up every last bit of root.

ROOT BALL: The roots and accompanying soil or compost when a plant is lifted from the open ground or removed from a container.

RUNNER: A horizontally spreading stem that runs across the ground and roots at the nodes to produces new plants. Often confused with a stolen.

SCARIFY: Scratching the outer surface of a lawn with a rake to increase water absorption and help germination; like giving it a good comb.

SEPAL: Part of the calyx, usually green and insignificant.

SETS: A young bulb or tuber with the capacity for producing a new plant.

SPECIES: A category in plant classification; the rank below genus that contains closely related individual plants.

STAMEN: The male floral organ, bearing an anther that produces pollen.

STIGMA: The female part of the flower that receives pollen.

STOLEN: A horizontally spreading stem that runs across the ground and roots at the tips to produces new plants. Often confused with a runner.

STOPPING: Removing the growing tip of a plant with the fingers to induce the growth of sideshoots and flowers. Also known as 'pinching out'.

STRATIFICATION: Storing seeds in warm or cold conditions to break dormancy and force germination.

STYLE: The part of the flower on which the stigma is carried.

TUBER: Root tubers include dahlias and have swollen roots at the base of the stem. They can be divided in spring by pulling them up and then cutting off individual roots, each with its own bud. Stem tubers, like potatoes, have 'eyes' and can be cut into several pieces for propagation purposes. Just make sure each piece has its own 'eye'.

VERMICULITE: A light potting material that looks like broken-up Styrofoam. Made from mica-like material, it holds water better than compost and is ideal for covering seeds.

The Seasons

A general guide to the seasons in Ireland and Britain

Spring

Early: February-March
Mid: March-April
Late: April-May

Summer

Early: May-June
Mid: June-July
Late: July-August

Autumn

Early: August-September
Mid/Late: September-November

Winter

Early/Mid: December-January
Late: January-February

Easy Plant Finder

(Or: common names and their Latin equivalent)

Amaryllis: Hippeastrum
Bamboo: Arundinaria
Bergamot: Monarda
Bluebell: Hyacinthoides
Box: Buxus
Broom: Cytisus
Buttercup: Ranunculus
Carnation: Dianthus
Catmint: Nepeta
Cineraria: Pericallis
Cinquefoil: Potentilla
Columbine: Aquilegia
Comfrey: Symphytum
Currant: Ribes
Daisy: Bellis
Daisy bush: Olearia
Dogwood: Cornus
Elder: Sambucus
Fennel: Foeniculum
Fig: Ficus
Flowering quince: Chaenomeles
Forget-me-not: Myosotis
Foxglove: Digitalis
Gorse: Ulex
Grape hyacinth: Muscari
Heather: Calluna, Erica
Holly: Ilex
Hollyhock: Alcea

Honeysuckle: Lonicera
Ivy: Hedera
Laurel: Prunus
Lily of the valley: Convallaria
Lilac: Syringa
Maple: Acer
Marigold: Calendula; Tagetes (African)
Michaelmas daisy: Aster
Mock orange: Philadelphus
Nasturtium: Tropaeolum
Oleaster: Elaeagnus
Pampas grass: Cortaderia
Peony: Paeonia
Pink: Dianthus
Poppy: Papaver; Eschscholzia (Californian), Glaucium
  (Horned), Mecanopsis (Himalayan)
Primrose: Primula
Privet: Ligustrum
Red hot poker: Kniphofia
Rock rose: Cistus
Sage: Salvia
St John's wort: Hypericum
Sea holly: Eryngium
Smoke tree: Cotinus
Snapdragon: Antirrhinum
Snowdrop: Galanthus
Speedwell: Veronica
Stock: Matthiola
Sumach: Rhus
Sunflower: Helianthus
Sweet Pea: Lathyrus
Tarragon: Artemisia

Tobacco plant: Nicotiana
Veronica: Hebe
Virginia creeper: Parthenocissu
Wallflower: Erysimum
Water lily: Nymphaea, Nuphar (American)
Willow: Salix
Witch-hazel: Hamamelis
Yew: Taxus

Further Reading

Most public libraries have an extensive collection of gardening books, many long out of print, but all of them worth a browse.

General

Reader's Digest New Encyclopedia of Garden Plants and Flowers (The Reader's Digest Association, London 2001). Not just an A to Z of every plant imaginable, written by a long list of contributors, this invaluable book also includes essays on a variety of gardening topics.

Royal Horticultural Society Gardening through the Year by Ian Spence (Dorling Kindersley, London, 2002). *Royal Horticultural Society Encyclopaedia of Gardening* ed. Christopher Brickell (Dorling Kindersley, London, 1993). *RHS Practical Guides: Roses* (and many other topics) (Dorling Kindersley, London, 1999). All RHS books are worth a look.

The Experts Series all by Dr D.G Hessayon (Expert Books, London, 1999). You will undoubtedly end up buying at least one volume from this cheap 'n' cheerful series, which can vary in quality. *The Tree and Shrub Expert* is one of the good ones.

Best Foliage Shrubs by Stefan Buczacki (Hamlyn, London, 1998). One of a series; refreshingly, Buczacki isn't afraid to voice his opinions.

The Mitchell Beazley Pocket Guide to Garden Plants by Hugh Johnson and Paul Miles (Mitchell Beazley, London, 1995). The Mitchell Beazley guide is cheap and includes (almost) every plant you can think of. Ideal for slipping into the pocket on a visit to the garden centre.

The Well-Tempered Garden by Christopher Lloyd (Weidenfeld & Nicolson, London 2001). A welcome reprint of a gardening classic.

Organic Gardening

Organic Gardening by Pauline Spears, Sue Stickland and the RHS (Mitchell Beazley, London 1999). Another worthwhile RHS book.

The Green Gardener's Handbook by Margaret Elphinstone and Julia Langley (Thorsons, Wellingborough, 1990). An excellent guide and an entertaining read, touching on matters such as the history of gardening and of the many plants we now enjoy.

Websites

About the best starting point is the 'Gardener's World' site at www.bbc.co.uk/gardening. For organic gardening, start with the Henry Doubleday Research Association site at www.hrda.org.uk.

Other sites

Links: www.gardenlinks.ndo.co.uk
Royal Horticultural Society www.rhs.org.uk
Soil Association www.soilassociation.org
Thompson & Morgan seeds www.Thompson-Morgan.com